THE ROSARY

THE ROSARY

keeping company with Jesus and Mary

KAREN EDMISTEN

PUBLISHED BY ST. ANTHONY MESSENGER PRESS
CINCINNATI, OHIO

Unless otherwise noted, Scripture passages have been taken from the *Revised Standard Version*, Catholic edition. Copyright 1946, 1952, 1971 by the Division of Christian Education of the National Council of Churches of Christ in the USA. Used by permission. All rights reserved.

Note: The editors of this volume have made minor changes in capitalization to some of the Scripture quotations herein. Please consult the original source for proper capitalization.

Quotations from Vatican II and papal documents are taken from the Vatican Web site, www.vatican.va.

Quotations are taken from the English translation of the *Catechism of the Catholic Church* for the United States of America (indicated as *CCC*), 2nd ed. Copyright 1997 by United States Catholic Conference—Libreria Editrice Vaticana.

Cover and book design by Jennifer Tibbits
Cover photo/image copyrightKrzysztof Slusarczyk/istockphoto

LIBRARY OF CONGRESS CATALOGING-IN-PUBLICATION DATA

Edmisten, Karen.
  The rosary : keeping company with Jesus and Mary / Karen Edmisten.
    p. cm.
  Includes bibliographical references.
  Rosary.
  ISBN 978-0-86716-875-4 (pbk. : alk. paper) 1. Catholic Church—
Prayers and devotions. I. Title.
  BX2163.E25 2009
  242'.74—dc22
                                        2009007152

ISBN 978-0-86716-875-4

Published by Servant Books, an imprint of St. Anthony Messenger Press
28 W. Liberty St.
Cincinnati, OH 45202
www.ServantBooks.org

Printed in the United States of America.

Printed on acid-free paper.

09 10 11 12 13 5 4 3 2 1

FOR ANDREA

Contents

ACKNOWLEDGMENTS

Thanks go first to God, without whom I'd still be an unhappy atheist. Thank you to Mother Mary, whose prayers sustain me, and to Papa John Paul the Great, for teaching me about "learning him."

To my beloved husband, Tom, enormous thanks for your heroic efforts in providing me with time to write and for your excellent editing skills and ideas. To my wonderful daughters, Emily, Lizzy and Kate, thank you for your cheerful support and sacrifices as I wrote this book. And thanks to my entire family and many friends for prayers and support.

To Jack Donnelly, Andrea Schlickbernd, Alice Gunther and Lissa Peterson, thanks for invaluable insights. Thank you, too, to Kathy Steffensmeier, Sister Marita Schweiger, Paula Lindstrom, Bridget O'Brien, Mary Ellen Barrett and Cindy Bishop. Thank you to Father Joe Taphorn for your direction and unflagging encouragement. And Jack, thanks for seeing the Catholic in me when all I could see was the darkness.

Thanks to Mike Aquilina. The Lord has seen fit to have our writing paths cross over the years, and I'm grateful for such a gift.

Finally, many thanks to Cynthia Cavnar and Lucy Scholand. I cannot imagine a better editing team, and I am indebted to you for your expertise and advice.

FOREWORD

It was probably as a zygote that I first grew familiar with the rosary. My mom was forty-seven when I was born, and I am the youngest of seven children. The rosary was a constant with her. I don't know if she ever finished all five decades in one sitting (or while standing or cleaning or cooking), but she often had her beads in hand or pocket, and my early life passed not to the rhythm of a clock but to the rhythm of the Hail Mary. From the beginning it was my element, as surely as Mom's cushion of amniotic fluid ever was.

Mom grew up in the decades immediately after the Marian apparitions at Fatima, Portugal, when even *The New York Times* displayed the rosary on its front pages. Once a year in her little ethnic parish near Scranton, Pennsylvania, the men carried a statue of Our Lady of the Rosary on their shoulders through the streets of the town. Father Patrick Peyton promoted the rosary on the radio, as Bishop Fulton Sheen later would on television. The rosary was Mom's element too, and she made sure it was ours.

I'm sorry to say that I did not pick up my mother's habits of prayer till I was a parent myself. Maybe it's because the wider culture had grown almost militantly secularist by the time I hit my teen years. Fathers Peyton and Sheen were not the presence they once had been, and radio and TV—never mind *The New York Times*—were busy broadcasting a different sort of "gospel."

Mom persevered though, praying for her children through the trials and crises of our adulthood. Once she was empty-nesting, I'll bet she occasionally got to pray a rosary all the way through. It was her most effective way of continuing to mother us.

When she was eighty-five, in the aftermath of major surgery, Mom suffered a stroke. The immediate effects were devastating. Mom recognized me only intermittently, which was far more difficult for me than I ever could have predicted. Till that moment (I was thirty-nine), I was sure I was the sun at the center of her solar system.

My siblings made sure Mom had her rosary with her at all times. For though she had lost so much, at least temporarily, she retained something important: She still knew how to move her fingers along the beads and say the prayers. That action had burned neural pathways that were, apparently, ineradicable. These proved to be the pathways to her healing. Her rosary was the lifeline by which she pulled herself (or was pulled) back to health.

As I write this, Mom is happily living at home at the age of ninety-one. She has a rich life, even though she's confined to a wheelchair. She loves to see her children and grandchildren and great-grandchildren, whom she knows and calls by name. She loves to play catch with the youngest of them. And she can still pray a mighty rosary.

All of Mom's life had been a remote preparation for her great ordeal, which was spiritual at least as much as it was medical. Can we doubt that we, too, will face such ordeals? Shouldn't we be preparing ourselves even now?

We can't count on the rosary-steeped culture my mom once knew, but we can still count on our beads, and we can make them as much a part of our being as my mom did.

Karen Edmisten wants us to do just that, and she's helping us as only a true mother can. In this book I recognize the loving guidance of a mother, of my mother and of Our Mother.

—MIKE AQUILINA

INTRODUCTION

I'm not an expert on the rosary, unless *expert* can be defined as "an average Catholic who prays the rosary and has found it to be powerful, comforting and worth talking about." I don't pretend to know everything there is to know about the rosary, and this book will not be a comprehensive history or an academic treatise. I won't try to convince you that you must pray the rosary every day (though that's a great idea). I won't tell you that every great saint has loved it (Saint Thérèse of Lisieux is known to have struggled mightily with it). I don't want to make you feel guilty if you don't like it, have never prayed it or haven't ever gotten the hang of meditating on the mysteries.

What I do hope to do is present a convincing case for a compelling prayer, clear up some common misunderstandings and offer some practical tips for this much-loved but ironically much-avoided prayer.

The rosary has been around for hundreds of years and has been associated with numerous miracles and apparitions of Mary. It has received her confirmation and encouragement and has offered hope, comfort, peace and increased faith to millions of people through the years and around the world. It's a prayer that simply doesn't go away.

At the same time the rosary is a prayer that many struggle with. Limited time, distractions, concern about meditations and legalistic approaches all conspire to make us worry instead of pray.

As a former atheist, I understand every worry that can accompany the rosary. It was once as foreign to me as hieroglyphics, as were all things religious. I certainly didn't believe in miracles, for example—not in the tiny ones that happen every day nor in the enormous miracles of the Incarnation and the Resurrection of Christ. When I finally began reading Scripture, I questioned why, after all those amazing biblical feats, there weren't any modern miracles. Like a petulant child, I challenged Jesus to appear on my doorstep and multiply loaves and fishes before my eyes. *That* would convince me he was real.

I shudder at my arrogance, but God, Father to even petulant little ones, *did* send miracles. The first was that he didn't give up on me when I was an anti-marriage, anti-child, pro-abortion know-it-all. In his infinite mercy he embraced this seemingly lost cause and never let go. He knocked relentlessly at my door. He gave me the gifts of undeserved grace, patient friends and good books. He let me hunger and thirst, and he hounded me until I couldn't resist.

Baptism (at the age of thirty) and reception into the Catholic Church (five years later) led to things I'd never have predicted. One of those things was a newfound belief in miracles of all sizes, including the miracle that I've grown to love a prayer—the rosary—that I once could barely comprehend.

In this book we'll take a closer look at all of the worries, hesitations and questions that can be our unwelcome companions in prayer and particularly in praying the rosary. And whether you're a cradle Catholic who grew up with the rosary, a convert who came to it late as I did or merely a curious onlooker, I hope this book can act as a primer, a reference and a source of support. It comes to you not from an expert but simply from a fellow traveler. Think of me as your friend on the journey, offering to share the best stops, the most nourishing refreshment and the most stunning miracles that she's found along the way.

chapter one

A SAFE PORT

O Blessed Rosary of Mary, sweet chain which unites us to God,
bond of love which unites us to the angels, tower of salvation
against the assaults of Hell, safe port in our universal shipwreck,
we will never abandon you.

—BLESSED BARTOLO LONGO[1]

Before I became a Catholic, I never used the phrase "Blessed
Mother." It sounded odd. The mother of Jesus was simply "Mary"
to me, if I bothered to think of her at all. Equally odd was the idea
that "Mary's prayer"—the rosary—could become a helpful or
beloved one. The words of Blessed Bartolo Longo, known as the
"apostle of the rosary," would have been incomprehensible to me.
I could see our fallen world as a shipwreck, but the notion that
the rosary was our safe port was foreign indeed.

Blessed Bartolo, a lay Dominican who lived in the 1800s,
endured his own disastrous shipwreck of a life, from which he was
mercifully, miraculously rescued. A former Satanist priest, Bartolo
experienced an amazing conversion, which he credited to the intercession of the Blessed Mother as well as to family and friends. He
wrote, "The Rosary is a teacher of life, a teacher full of gentleness
and love, where people beneath the gaze of Mary, almost without
noticing, discover they are being slowly educated in preparation

for the second life, that which is authentic life, for it is not destined to end in a very few years, but to go on unto eternity."[2]

Though I now appreciate the truth and beauty of those words, I also remember the many years they were out of my grasp. My own conversion was not as dramatic as that of a former Satanist, but my entry into the Catholic Church obviously represented a radical departure from my life as an atheist. And like Blessed Bartolo Longo, I credit in large part the intercession of our Blessed Mother and friends who prayed "Mary's prayer" for me.

I remember when I first tried to pray the rosary. Any formal recitation of prayer was alien to me, and I had questions about all kinds of prayers, especially the rosary. I wasn't yet worried about such things as the level of my meditation or the depth of my contemplation or whatever I was supposed to call it. No, I needed to know some more fundamental things, or so it seemed to my panicked self. Now that I was actually becoming a Catholic, I wanted to "do it right," and I didn't have all the answers.

What were my questions?

In his explanation of the rosary, a friend had casually said, "Announce the first mystery." I nodded to mask my confusion, but later I dug up some instructions on the rosary to clarify. They said the same thing. So now I had to know what it meant to "announce" a mystery. Did I have to say something out loud? Was I announcing something to God? Was I supposed to pray the rosary only with other people, when things could be announced?

I was terribly worried about praying the rosary "incorrectly" and about looking foolish in front of other Catholics. Why couldn't I remember the entire Apostles' Creed? What if I left out a few Hail Marys or forgot the words to that prayer at the end? Myriad anxieties arose as I tried to pray this supposedly peaceful prayer.

I did eventually move beyond those problems. First, I realized that "announcing" really just means "focusing." That is, I can name a mystery out loud, if praying with others, but when alone I can simply hold the thought in my mind.

But with such mechanics behind me, I ran headlong into new quandaries. Distraction, boredom and apprehension about "how I was doing" (and about why I got so sleepy during my prayers) threatened to derail my new devotion. As I finished a rosary with "Hail, Holy Queen" and uttered the words "To thee do we cry," I wanted to cry in frustration at my failure to do the rosary justice.

I've learned that I'm not alone. It seems that the rosary, more than any other Catholic prayer, elicits an astounding number of anxieties. And yet many of us return to it despite our struggles. Why?

I think we cling to the rosary because, on some level, we not only sense the beauty of the prayer but also see and feel its efficacy. Even when we're frustrated by our execution of it, we know that somehow it works. It is powerful. It connects us to Mary, and it is a direct line to her Son, Jesus.

So we persevere, ask our questions and whisper cautiously to friends whom we suspect might also fall asleep while praying. We fumble, but we learn—even all the words to the Apostles' Creed. Then one day we realize that we are indeed doing it "right" or, at least, "better." We're praying with more purpose and gratitude, maybe even with a deeper sense of joy. And the rosary is doing what it was meant to do in the first place: It's drawing us nearer to the one it's ultimately all about, Jesus Christ.

Since my conversion my quest to do the rosary justice has led me to sublime mountaintops and down into parched valleys, with predictable plateaus along the way. The rosary has seen me through miscarriages and births, motherhood, the amazing conversion of my husband, moves, new homes and losses. It has accompanied me on mundane tasks and through Herculean challenges. It has been, in one form or another, my companion since I claimed the name "Catholic."

The rosary is an ancient and beautiful prayer, rich in layers, pregnant with possibilities and abundantly overflowing with the means to draw us closer to the Son of the one whose intercession we ask. And while the journey has convinced me that Mary will always intercede for me, if in sometimes surprising ways, one thing remains the same: It's up to me to actually pray what Pope John Paul II called his "favourite prayer."[3]

Let's take a closer look now at how to do that. We'll see how the rosary fits into our modern, busy lives and our sometimes shipwrecked world. Perhaps the rosary can become your safe port too, a gift from our Blessed Mother.

chapter two

THE ROSARY

ITS ORIGINS AND ITS MIRACLES

To recite the Rosary is nothing other than to contemplate *with Mary the face of Christ.*

—POPE JOHN PAUL II, *Rosarium Virginis Mariae,* 3

What is the rosary? It's a simple question, though the answer can get surprisingly complicated. Let's start with the basics.

The rosary is a popular prayer. It is a chaplet, which is a devotion that uses a string of beads to keep track of a certain number of prayers. Structurally the rosary is made up of five simple sets of repeated prayers, with each set made up of an Our Father and ten Hail Marys. Each set is called a "decade" for the ten Hail Marys. And each decade has been assigned a "mystery," an episode from the life of Christ or Mary on which we meditate while saying the prayers.

And that's it. That's the essence of the rosary.

It is called a "rosary" for several possible reasons, which relate both to practicalities and to the Blessed Mother. First, some early prayer beads may actually have been made from rose petals. Second, some people like to think of the circle of prayers as a crown (a word that shares origins with the word *chaplet*) that can be presented to Mary as a gift of prayer. A popular name for Mary is the "Mystical Rose." Connect these ideas—a crown, a chaplet of prayers counted on rose petal beads (which also form a circle), presented to Mary, the Mystical Rose—and it's not surprising that the devotion eventually came to be called a rosary.

So the rosary is a popular, bead-counting prayer that's made up of Hail Marys. But that doesn't tell us much, does it? Why the beads, anyway, and what has made the rosary so popular? What does it offer that other prayers don't? And where did it come from in the first place?

While it's not my intention to offer an in-depth history of the rosary, it will be helpful to take a closer look at the origins of the prayer before we move on.

A Brief History of the Rosary

Ask a handful of Catholics where the rosary came from, and you'll get a handful of answers.

Many of us have heard that Saint Dominic received the prayer directly from the Blessed Mother in the twelfth century, with an exhortation to pray it in order to combat heretical beliefs of the time. Those who have dug further into history may say that before Saint Dominic, the seeds of the rosary were planted by monks who prayed the psalms (all 150 of them) and kept track of their prayers with beads, pebbles or knotted strings. Those psalms later metamorphosed into 150 Our Fathers for the benefit of illiterate lay brothers who could not participate in reading and praying Scripture. Eventually the "Psalter of Mary," or the repetition of 150 Hail Marys, was prayed in the same way.

There is evidence to suggest that something like the rosary predates even those developments. Many religions have a history of some sort of prayer that is counted on beads.

But let's return to Saint Dominic. Certainly the Order of Preachers, which Saint Dominic founded in the 1200s (thus the nickname "Dominicans"), did a tremendous amount to spread devotion to Mary and the rosary. In *Saint Dominic: The Grace of the Word*, Father Guy Bedouelle tells us that Saint Dominic and his brothers prayed the Hail Mary with frequency and with fervent devotion. At that time the prayer would have consisted only of its first two lines: "Hail Mary, full of grace. The Lord is with you."[1]

Father Bedouelle chronicles other evolutions that occurred during the Middle Ages. He notes the psalms' metamorphosis into the 150 Our Fathers and later the Psalter of Mary. He explains that religious began to meditate on the mysteries of Mary's life in order to enrich their prayer. "They were eager for the concrete, for pictures; anxious to see and to count; they would neglect no possible means of calling to mind the things of God."[2]

The oft-told story of the appearance of Mary to Saint Dominic, in which she gave him a rosary, possibly originated in the *Rosarium*, a Marian poem written in the fourteenth century, which wove together numerous and varied stories about Dominic and the Blessed Mother. Among those stories was one in which Dominic experienced a vision of Mary, the "Virgin of Mercy," covering and protecting his Dominican brothers with her mantle. Dominic, profoundly moved by the vision, preached to his brothers of Mary's love and maternal care and exhorted them to deeper Marian devotion.[3]

Alan de la Roche, a Dominican of the fifteenth century, did a great deal to spread devotion to the rosary.[4] He's also known to have deferred credit to the much-beloved Saint Dominic, probably in recognition of Dominic's profound love for Mary. Another Dominican of that century, Jacques Sprenger, is credited with the later separation of the mysteries into joyful, sorrowful and glorious categories.[5]

None of this is to say that the "credit" given to Saint Dominic was unjustified. Father Bedouelle makes this important point:

> [W]e can realize what medieval men were trying to do by attributing the invention of the Rosary to Saint Dominic. They wanted, in their poetic way, to express the power of prayer in which the Founder so confidently believed, and the role of the Virgin in salvation history.…
>
> It was fitting that Dominic, in his Marian devotion, which was inseparable from his apostolic zeal, should be thus represented in the beatitude he had so ardently announced."[6]

If Saint Dominic's role was somewhat magnified by his brothers, that would seem a conscious choice made out of love for their founder, who did indeed experience a life-changing vision of the Blessed Mother. While the vision and the invention of the rosary may not have happened in exactly the way pious tradition describes, clearly Saint Dominic's Order of Preachers played an enormous role in the propagation of the rosary and continues to encourage and spread this devotion today. So it's legitimate to say that Saint Dominic gave us the gift and legacy of the rosary.

MIRACULOUS CONFIRMATIONS

The Blessed Mother herself has affirmed and encouraged the rosary a number of times, especially over the last two centuries. Not surprisingly for a mother, two of her most powerful affirmations came to us through children. And those affirmations were associated with miraculous events.

In Lourdes, France, in 1858, the Blessed Mother appeared to a simple, uneducated but immensely faithful girl from a very poor family, fourteen-year-old Bernadette Soubirous. In the first vision the Blessed Mother held a beautiful rosary, and young Bernadette, though confused and fumbling, did her best to pray along. Mary appeared to Bernadette eighteen times over a period of several months, and although no one else ever saw the virgin, witnesses said that Bernadette seemed practically transfigured as she prayed during the visions.

Bernadette later entered religious life. She died twenty-one years after the apparitions, and her body lies incorrupt to this day in a glass casket in Nevers, France. Miracles of healing have since been associated with the waters of Lourdes.

In 1917 in Fatima, Portugal, three young children—named Francisco, Jacinta and Lucia—had a stunning experience. The Blessed Virgin Mary appeared to them, urging them to pray the rosary every day for peace. She also gave them a new prayer: "O my Jesus, forgive us our sins. Save us from the fires of hell; lead all souls to heaven, especially those in most need of thy mercy." Many people have since adopted this "Fatima Prayer" as part of their rosary recitation.

Miracles have been associated with Fatima as well, from the time of the apparitions and since. Thousands of people witnessed the "miracle of the sun" on October 13, 1917, in which the sun appeared to dance and fall to earth. This miracle had been predicted by the children, based on what Mary had told them.

The Church does not require the faithful to believe in either of these appearances or in any other Marian apparition (or private revelation of any kind, for that matter). The Catholic Church teaches that public revelation (or "all that we need to know in order to get to heaven," which is also called "the deposit of faith") came to a close with Jesus and the canon of the New Testament. However, both Fatima and Lourdes have been declared "approved apparitions." This means that the Church has deemed them *worthy* of belief.

Accounts of the events and associated miracles all attest to the supernatural nature of these encounters, which revolve around the Blessed Mother's special prayer, the rosary. And at Fatima Mary called herself "Our Lady of the Rosary."[7]

Further miraculous confirmation of the rosary's power is associated with the Feast of Our Lady of the Rosary. This feast, celebrated on October 7, was instituted by Pope Saint Pius V, a Dominican (we see the order's enduring influence), following a different type of miracle. Christians battling the Turkish army at the seemingly hopeless Battle of Lepanto in 1571 rallied to a decisive victory after the pope called on the faithful to intercede with prayer and fasting. "[A]t the very hour that the contest was raging, the procession of the rosary in the church of the Minerva [in Rome] was pouring forth petitions for victory."[8]

One need only skim books and Web sites on the rosary to see that countless miracles, large and small, are attributed to Our Lady's intercession. Pope Pius IX is said to have stated, "Among all the devotions approved by the Church, none has been so favored by so many miracles as the devotion of the Most Holy Rosary."[9]

In summary, we can say that although the history of the rosary is something of a patchwork, some things are indisputable. Those devoted both to Mary and to furthering the kingdom of her Son have fervently promoted the rosary. And Our Lady herself has miraculously encouraged it as a powerful prayer for the salvation of souls and for peace in the world.

But why all the Hail Marys? Is it really easier to grow close to Christ through rote prayer than through spontaneous prayer?

chapter three

BEYOND WORDS

Without [contemplation] the Rosary is a body without a soul, and its recitation is in danger of becoming a mechanical repetition of formulas and of going counter to the warning of Christ: "And in praying do not heap up empty phrases as the Gentiles do; for they think that they will be heard for their many words" (Mt. 6:7).

—POPE PAUL VI, *Marialis Cultus,* 47

Why does the Church encourage a form of prayer that is so repetitious and that can therefore appear meaningless?

A vital thing I've learned during my Catholic years is that in formal prayer, the form contributes to the substance, rather than subtracting from it. Let's take a look at the Mass, for example.

I remember going to Mass with a friend long before I became a Catholic. One of my objections at the time was that the liturgy seemed cold and mechanical. From the outside looking in, I could see only automatons mechanically reciting prayers and droning responses. "How can this possibly have any purpose," I wondered, "when it's not from the heart? It's meaningless, isn't it?"

Granted, a sea of voices simultaneously reciting the same prayers can sound mechanical, but my assumption was both naïve and presumptuous. I couldn't possibly have known what was happening in the hearts and minds of all those present at the Masses I attended. This was confirmed for me when, after becoming a Catholic, my own voice "droned" while my heart was bursting with passion for God.

While responses during the Mass come "automatically" and are prescribed, that does not render them meaningless for us. The prayers of the Mass provide a structure that frees us to experience worship more fully, precisely because we can rely on the stability of the form. Rather than wondering what to do next, we have the basics down. We know when to stand, when to kneel, when to respond. As C.S. Lewis noted in *Letters to Malcolm, Chiefly on Prayer,* an ever-changing liturgy can distract from its purpose: "Try as one may to exclude it, the question 'What on earth is he up to now?' will intrude. It lays one's devotion waste."[1]

The rosary's prescribed form gives the prayer a shape that frees our mind for the meditations that are meant to accompany it. There is a beginning, a middle and an end. That form allows us to focus. It is the springboard from which the mental prayer takes off.

VAIN REPETITION?

Let's look at the warning in Scripture: "And in praying do not heap up empty phrases as the Gentiles do; for they think that they will be heard for their many words" (Matthew 6:7). Are we "heaping up empty phrases" when we pray the rosary?

"Vain" repetition is meaningless repetition, done for its own sake. If I believe that my salvation will depend on an accounting of my prayer quantity, then I may indeed be tempted to heap up a mountain of empty phrases. But as notable as those efforts would be for a world record, they would also, without a doubt, be in vain. God is not in the business of keeping such accounts.

Why then do we repeat the prayers of the rosary so many times?

As we just said, the rosary's form contributes to its substance. The repetition is the frame, or the foundation, upon which the structure of meditation is built. The repetition isn't meaningless but serves a vital purpose. It's the backbone of the prayer, the skeletal support for its real heart and soul.

It's also important to note that Jesus did not say that we must avoid *all* repetition. He said that we are to avoid "empty" repetition. Practically speaking, it would be impossible to avoid all repetition in prayer. We can pray the same prayer countless times in a day, a week, a month or a year, and the prayer does not lose its power with each utterance. Rather, every instance of sincere prayer is an expression of confidence in and love for God.

When Jesus gave us the Lord's Prayer, he did not expect us to say it once and be done with it. And in Revelation the "great multitude in heaven" repeat *Hallelujahs* to the Lord in praise and worship (see Revelation 19:1–6). Is this repetition in vain? Or is it an intense expression of worship, worthy praise of the Lamb of God?

Recently a friend related this story to me. His friend's son was in intensive care after being hit by a drunk driver. This mother would kneel before the Lord and pray, "Please, God, help him. Please, God, please, God, please, God, help him."

One day the mother realized that her prayers were, in one sense, nothing more than "repetition." Yet her intense plea rose up from deep within her soul. In her fear and desperation, she didn't know how else to pray.

I'm certain that in her heart and mind she held various pictures of her son: injured, helpless, frightened and in need, then perhaps healing and smiling and finally fully healed by God. Her mother's heart was assuredly "meditating" on these images as her voice repeated, "Please, God, help him."

Was her repetition empty? Hardly. It was a cry sent from the pit of despair to the throne of heaven, borne of surrender and trust. Her repetitious pleas were the foundation that supported the images of hope held in her heart.

I've found that my own informal, spontaneous prayers are not necessarily less repetitious or more profound than formal prayers. How often I repeat the same pleas to God and offer redundant lists of petitions!

The rosary is the same. While it could certainly appear to be vain or empty, properly approached it is a prayer from the heart, a cry from the soul and a way to rejoice in the glory of our salvation. The "fixed form" that frees our mind, that very repetition, is necessary for our focus. It's what allows the cries of anguish or shouts of joy to rise up and find voice. Repetition becomes an anchor that fastens our minds to the prayer and keeps our thoughts from floating far away.

So is it enough just to say my Our Fathers and Hail Marys and be done with it for the day? The short answer is, "No. Sorry. It's better than nothing, but it's not enough." The long answer is that although recitation of the prayers *is* better than nothing, we will gain immeasurably more from the rosary if we incorporate meditation. Yes, the rosary is a prescribed set of prayers, but it is more than the sum of those parts. As we just saw, the prescription is there to help us focus. Once we're focused, the real prayer can begin.

MEDITATION

Consider for a moment the history we discussed. When the monks prayed the psalms, they entered deeply into Scripture and into the story of our salvation. The book of Psalms is an astounding chronicle of human emotion and experience, of joyful praise and agonizing despair, of divine intervention and man's response. The psalms are about our relationship with the Lord. When meditation on the psalms was eliminated (for the sake of the illiterate), something vital was lost. It's simply not the same thing to pray the Our Father 150 times as it is to immerse oneself in the richness of the book of Psalms.

That is *not* to say that the Our Father is meaningless when prayed without added meditation. No prayer is ever meaningless. And the Our Father is practically a stand-alone catechism of our faith, rich and profound. Prayers, which are essentially sacramentals (sacred signs, symbols or objects that dispose us to receive grace), are always valuable in and of themselves.

Yet it seems to me that the later addition of meditations to the rosary was a recognition of (and remedy for) what had been lost. Meditation restored the purpose of the prayers, allowing us once again to enter deeply into and meditate on Scripture and salvation history, this time with an added bonus: the intercession of our Blessed Mother.

Meditating on Christ's life through the mysteries of the rosary cannot help but draw us closer to him. Meditation is a quest for deeper understanding (see *CCC*, 2705), and in praying the rosary, we are on a quest to know Jesus more intimately. Admittedly, the quality of our quest will vary, as time and circumstances allow, but we should always remember that the rosary is not a set of prayers to race through every day. Rather, the core of the rosary is meditation.

CLOSER TO JESUS

Pope John Paul II zeroed in on the Christ-centered nature of the rosary when he observed something very basic about the tool we use to pray it: the beads. He noted that they all *"converge upon the*

Crucifix."[2] In other words, Jesus Christ is at the beginning and the end of the prayer. He is the essence of the meditations. All things point to him, including the simple tool we use to aid us in our contemplation.

There's nothing mysterious about the fact that the mysteries are the key to the rosary. The mysteries, mini-portraits of the life of Jesus, come to us from Scripture. They are what make the prayer Christ-centered. It really is all about him.

Because the rosary is anchored in Christ, it cannot help but draw us closer to him. To pray the rosary is to spend time with Jesus. It is a walk with him through every facet of his life, from his earthly conception to the glory of his Resurrection. The rosary is the life of Christ in microcosm. One who prays the rosary regularly is keeping company with the Lord.

Pope John Paul II, shortly after his election to the papacy, aptly summed it up this way:

> Against the background of the words *Ave Maria* the principal events of the life of Jesus Christ pass before the eyes of the soul. They take shape in the complete series of the joyful, sorrowful and glorious mysteries, and they put us in living communion with Jesus through—we might say—the heart of his Mother. At the same time our heart can embrace in the decades of the Rosary all the events that make up the lives of individuals, families, nations, the Church, and all mankind. Our personal concerns and those of our neighbour, especially those who are closest to us, who are dearest to us. Thus the simple prayer of the Rosary marks the rhythm of human life.[3]

chapter four

HAIL MARY

The centre of gravity in the Hail Mary, the hinge as it were which joins its two parts, is *the name of Jesus.*

—POPE JOHN PAUL II, *Rosarium Virginis Mariae,* 33

In your experience with the rosary, you may have wondered about some of the same things I did in my early encounters. First of all, perhaps you've questioned why, if the rosary is so Christ-centered, it seems to be all about Mary. Second, you may be curious about praying to Mary. Is that what we're doing, and is it a form of idolatry?

In the last chapter I mentioned Pope John Paul II's observation that all the beads of the rosary *"converge upon the Crucifix"*[1] as an indicator that the rosary is truly about Christ. But if it's about him, why do we focus so much on Mary? Where is Jesus in this prayer? Other than a brief mention ("blessed is the fruit of thy womb, Jesus"), he's nowhere to be found, is he?

ALL ABOUT MARY?

If you are inclined to think that Jesus doesn't make much of an appearance in the Hail Mary, it is helpful to remember the difference between an implied presence and an explicitly stated one. Consider some of the central doctrines of our faith that, at first glance, don't seem to make an appearance in the Bible.

The Trinity is an excellent example. The word *Trinity* simply doesn't appear in Scripture. It took many years, a number of Church councils, extensive wrangling and a great deal of discernment to decide just which word best summed up "God the Father, God the Son and God the Holy Spirit." And yet the Trinity is present throughout the entire Old and New Testaments (see *CCC*, 237).

In the Old Testament, for example, we see a hint of the Holy Spirit in Genesis 1:2: "And the Spirit of God was moving over the face of the waters." We also see the Trinity as the "us" in Genesis 1:26: "Then God said, 'Let us make man in our image, after our likeness.'"

It's an implicit presence of the Trinity, rather than an explicitly stated one, but thanks to the Church's teaching and guidance in this matter, we've been led to a fuller understanding of the nature of God. We can see the presence of the Son and the Holy Spirit from the beginning, even if they are not named as such in relation to the Father until later (see *CCC*, 249–256). In the same way Jesus is present, implicitly at first, then explicitly, in the Hail Mary.

Let's take a look, line by line.

"Hail Mary, full of grace." The first words of the Hail Mary come directly from Scripture. In Luke 1:28 the archangel Gabriel greets Mary: "Hail, full of grace."

We Catholics are so accustomed to this phrase that we take it for granted. At first glance it seems like a simple greeting, a mere fact, a recognition of Mary's state as we understand it. We know that Mary was immaculately conceived (that is, without the stain of original sin). The Lord prepared her for her unique role in salvation history by saving her before she was even born. "Yup," we Catholics say, "she's grace-filled."

But on second thought, that's astounding news. Excuse me? *Full* of grace? What other human being can claim that? No one else has been or ever will be "full of grace" in quite the same way that Mary was. The rest of us, having entered the world with original sin, can cling to those precious times when our souls are cleansed: at baptism and after each worthy confession. But we've never been in Mary's shoes. She was—think of it—*full* of grace. And it was only by the grace of God (including Jesus, the Second Person of the Trinity) that she could be so. There's the first appearance of Jesus in the Hail Mary.

"The Lord is with thee." Gabriel's words to Mary in the second half of Luke 1:28 assure Mary (and us) that God is present, and that again includes the Second Person of the Trinity, who will become the incarnate Jesus. He prepared her for her role from the moment of her conception. But soon the Second Person of the Trinity will also literally and physically be with Mary, dwelling within her womb. Jesus will be with her in a new and spectacular way.

"Blessed art thou among women." This is also scriptural: Elizabeth proclaims Mary's blessedness in Luke 1:42.

Mary was blessed among all women not through any merit of her own but by the grace of God. God chose her, ordaining that she would be conceived immaculately and made ready for his Son. She was blessed by this initial preparation and was further blessed at that sacred moment when the Lord asked for her *fiat*, her yes to his unprecedented request of her. She continued to be blessed in a singular way throughout her life as she lived out the privilege of mothering our Lord.

"And blessed is the fruit of thy womb, Jesus." Ah, there he is! In this line, also from Luke 1:42, Elizabeth acknowledges that Mary will be the mother of the holy one. He has been an integral part of the prayer from the first line, but now he is named.

"Holy Mary, Mother of God, pray for us sinners now and at the hour of our death." In this final section of the prayer, we refer to Mary as holy (made so by God) and as the Mother of God (which we'll delve into more fully later), and we request Mary's intercession. But such respect for and recognition of Mary's holiness, obedience and unique role don't make the prayer "about" her any more than my request for a respected neighbor's intercession makes my prayers about him.

So is the Hail Mary all about Mary, or is it about Jesus? Let's see what we've discovered so far.

PRAYER AND RELATIONSHIP

We've seen that Jesus is present throughout the Hail Mary. He is the reason behind Mary's holiness. In the presence of our Lord, we ask his mother for her intercession. The prayer then is not so much about *Mary* as it is about *her relationships*: her relationship with Jesus and her relationship with us.

First we are presented with Mary's perfect discipleship (and her unique relationship with Jesus), and then we make a plea for that perfectly devoted disciple to go to him with our prayers. That doesn't make the prayer any less God-centered. It actually *adds* to our understanding of what God calls all of us to be (holy disciples) and to do (turn to him in prayer for ourselves and others).

While not a perfect parallel, let's compare the Hail Mary to the Lord's Prayer. The Our Father is full of references to "us." We pray, "Give *us* our daily bread, forgive *us* as we forgive others, lead *us* not into temptation, deliver *us* from evil." And yet we don't find ourselves claiming, "Oh, that self-centered Our Father! It's all about us and not about God!" No, the Our Father is about *our relationship with God and with others.*

The Lord's Prayer is not about us at the expense of God. Neither is the Hail Mary about Mary at the expense of Jesus. Both prayers are about God's children in relation to him and to one another.

Prayer is always a conversation, a give-and-take within the context of a relationship. If there's no relationship, there's no real prayer. In the Hail Mary we recognize God's unique relationship with Mary and look upon her supreme example of obedience and fidelity. There we find an example from which we can learn.

So the answer to "Is it all about Mary?" is a firm no—and an equally firm yes. The prayer is *not* about Mary in the sense that it asks us to focus on her at the expense of our Lord. God is the foundation and backbone of the prayer, the reason for it and the one to whom we pray. On the other hand, it *is* about Mary in that it leads us to meditate on her relationship with God and thus on our own relationship with him. It helps us focus on what a wholly devoted disciple looks like. It inspires us to ponder what it must have been like to be "full of grace" and helps us contemplate Mary's freely given *fiat*, her certain (if trembling) "Yes, Lord."

And in the process we have the opportunity to grow closer to this extraordinary blessed woman, this saint above all saints. In short, the Hail Mary provides us with a model of discipleship as it draws us into a relationship with the Mother of God and with God himself.

And it's fitting that we *should* seek a relationship with Mary, because that is exactly what Jesus wants us to do. We do so not at the expense of our Lord but out of love for him. At Jesus' command from the cross, Mary accepted a maternal role for all of God's children.

Scripture tells us, "When Jesus saw his mother, and the disciple whom he loved standing near, he said to his mother, 'Woman, behold, your son!' Then he said to the disciple, 'Behold, your mother!' And from that hour the disciple took her to his own home" (John 19:26–27). Jesus "gave" John to Mary, as a son. He "gave" Mary to John, to be a mother. We, too, should follow the command of Jesus and behold our mother, given to us by our Lord himself. We have been honored with the privilege of taking Christ's beloved mother into our own hearts and homes.

Such relationships and connections are what the communion of saints is all about. We are told by the Church, "Until the Lord shall come in His majesty, and all the angels with Him and death being destroyed, all things are subject to Him, some of His disciples are exiles on earth, some having died are purified, and others are in glory" (*Lumen Gentium*, 49). In other words, we are all connected, whether we are part of the Church Militant (on earth), the Church Suffering (in purgatory) or the Church Triumphant (those in heaven). We are one body and one group of souls who can love and pray for one another. And if Mary is connected to us in this way, it is fitting that we should nurture our relationship with her and seek her prayers.

Do We Worship Mary?

Do we believe that we should worship "Holy Mary, Mother of God"? The quick answer is "Certainly not!"

As I mentioned previously, Mary's holiness came from the grace of God. She did not claim to be (nor does the Catholic Church declare her to be) holy through any merit of her own. Like the rest of us, she needed a Savior. God simply chose to save her in a unique way that he reserved only for the mother of Jesus.

It's important that we not confuse the words we use to explain these concepts, starting with *holy* and *divine*.

- *Holiness* comes to us only by the grace of God. It begins with baptism, when we are cleansed of original sin and made children of God. After that God continues to sanctify us, or make us holy, through our participation in the sacraments: Holy Communion, confirmation, confession, anointing of the sick, holy matrimony and holy orders. We all want to be holy and should strive continually to grow in holiness. God calls us to nothing less than being sanctified and remade, to grow continually closer to an eternity with him in heaven.

Divinity, on the other hand, refers to *being* God. Mary is certainly holy (as are all the saints in heaven, *saint* meaning "holy one of God"), but she is not divine.

We all have friends we feel are excellent examples for us. They are the people who are so close to God that we want to find out more about how they pray, how they order their days, what they think, read and do and where their spiritual journeys began. We're curious because we want to be as close to God as they are. When we strive to learn more about them and their methods, we're trying not to replace Jesus with our friends but to reach him with their help.

The same is true of Mary. Growing closer to Mary and learning from her discipleship are ways of growing closer to God. The Blessed Mother *always* points humbly to her beloved Son.

There are other terms about which we should be precise as well. Specifically, we don't want to confuse *worship* with *reverence.* The Catholic Church is meticulous in defining such terms. As an atheist I used to mock this precision as hair-splitting legalism. Now I can see how using precise terminology helps us sidestep a lot of confusion and get to the pertinent points.

Worship, according to the glossary of the *Catechism of the Catholic Church,* is "adoration and honor given to God."[2] Worship is reserved to God alone. *Latria* (derived from Greek) is the term the Church uses to refer to the worship that is due God. The word is *not* to be employed for any created being.

There are, however, additional terms, also derived from Greek, for other kinds of reverence that refer specifically to respect. Defined and acceptable forms of reverence for created beings include *dulia* and *hyperdulia*. *Dulia* is the respect that is due the saints and angels. *Hyperdulia* is the respect due the Mother of God.

Confusion can arise because *dulia*, *hyperdulia* and *latria* are all referred to as forms of veneration. But there is a strict line between veneration as respect for created beings and veneration as worship of God. If we speak of "venerating the saints and Mary" and in the next breath of "venerating God," it may sound as if we are worshipping all of them, but we're talking about different things.

Similarly, because Catholics sing songs about and say prayers "to" Mary, it can appear to non-Catholics that we worship her. Perhaps that's because many non-Catholic forms of worship center on prayer and music. Some non-Catholics assume that "prayer + music = worship."

We Catholics see (and verbally express) worship differently. Prayer and music are *part* of the Mass, for example, but the heart of worship in the Holy Sacrifice of the Mass is the Eucharist. Nothing and no one equals or supersedes our Lord. So we can pay a proper level of respect, even through music and in prayers, to created beings, but that respect is not the equivalent of worship *(latria)*, any more than singing a romantic love song leads to the worship of a spouse.

When we thus clarify our terms, we can see that there is no confusion for a Catholic about whom we worship. It is God alone.

Make no mistake: The Catholic Church forbids the worship of Mary. She condemns it as idolatry. There is only one God, and Mary is not he.

chapter five

THE *M*OTHER'S *P*LACE

> No one has ever devoted himself to the contemplation of the
> face of Christ as faithfully as Mary.
>
> —POPE JOHN PAUL II, *Rosarium Virginis Mariae*, 10

The Church affirms that we are to give the mother of our Lord
the respect she deserves, which was foretold in Luke 1:48, "All generations will call me blessed." And simply put, why would we not
wish to offer her love, honor and respect? Mary surrendered herself completely to all that accompanied bringing our Savior into
the world, including intense suffering. Seeking to emulate her
faith is not an act of worship; it is an act of learning from another
disciple. We should pay attention to that.

Some, however, might ask if we really need to pay quite so
much attention to it. Before I became a Catholic, I wondered the
same thing. If Mary was merely human, as we are, aren't we wast-
ing our time with so much emphasis on her?

First let's talk about being "merely" human. To our Lord
human beings aren't "merely" anything. God made us *in his image
and likeness*. He gave us an intellect and a will, intending us to use
those gifts to follow him and be with him forever. Before the fall
Adam and Eve were the perfect icons of what God wanted
humanity to be. In exercising their free will, they fell, and we have

inherited their fallen nature. But even now we are not disposable to God. We are still the love of his life, albeit stubborn, ignorant loves who don't often give him all that he deserves. He has given everything for us, including the gift of a new example: a perfect human disciple (Mary is often called "the new Eve").

To emphasize Mary's obedience is a waste of time only if we think God's choice is a waste of time. He, after all, was the one who chose Mary. He crafted a pure and holy vessel to bring our Lord into the world in a fitting manner and to give us the hope that true discipleship is possible. That alone inspires awe, doesn't it? And it leads us to honor Mary.

Think of how we naturally want to honor our own mothers and the mothers of those we love. We wouldn't dream of discounting the roles of these women: "Well, yes, she gave birth to me, but she wasn't really that important in the overall scheme of things." We'd be ashamed of ourselves if we dismissed our mothers as mere utilitarian vessels who delivered us into the world. On a much greater level, we cannot dismiss Mary as simply a cog in the machine. The Church reminds us not to discount her role.

If we love Jesus we will also love his mother. She is the shining example of what he wants us all to become. Honor and respect are the least we owe to the mother of the one who saves us. In honoring Mary we are honoring God's choice.

And when I contemplate Mary, that ordinary yet extraordinary woman who physically cared for Jesus each day—nursed him, held him, wiped his brow, picked him up when he fell down, fed him, watched him learn to walk and talk, rocked him in her arms and then watched him suffer and die for all mankind—I grasp, with renewed awe, her unparalleled relationship with him and her determination to fulfill her sacred duty.

MOTHER OF GOD

Just as the Church had to hammer out an acceptable way to express the doctrine of the Trinity, there was a lot of wrangling over the phrase "Mother of God" or *Theotokos*. But in AD 431 the Council of Ephesus affirmed that Mary was indeed and could be rightly called the Mother of God (see *CCC*, 495). This was in answer to the heresy of Nestorius, who argued that Mary could not be called "the God bearer" (or "Mother of God") because she could be the mother only of Jesus the man. This interpretation of the Incarnation logically leads to a separation of Jesus into two persons, rather than one divine person with two natures.

Nestorianism argued that calling Mary the Mother of God somehow inflated her position to one above and beyond God. The title and the doctrine, in reality, do no such thing. (And the Church doesn't want us to do such a thing. Remember, the Church is consistent in condemning the worship of Mary.) The title simply acknowledges the truth: Mary is "the mother of the eternal Son of God made man, who is God himself" (*CCC*, 509). She is not simply the mother of a human "part" of Jesus. She carried him—body, blood, soul and divinity—in her womb. She really and truly became his mother.

And perhaps that simple word *became* helps clear up the confusion. There was a time in Mary's life, prior to the Incarnation, when she was not the mother of Jesus. In other words, she does not and never did predate the Second Person of the Trinity. At God's appointed time she *became* the mother of Jesus, who *is* God. So calling Mary the "Mother of God" does not elevate her to a level above our Lord. It simply acknowledges a fact of God's plan.

And Scripture itself employs the phrase when Mary is greeted by Elizabeth, who calls her "the mother of my Lord" (Luke 1:43).

Elizabeth surely was not guilty of idolatry in applying this title to Mary. She recognized the astounding role Mary had been asked to play in our salvation.

To summarize, the Catholic Church does not want or attempt to take anything away from God in its recognition of Mary's role. The Church does, however, want to increase our understanding of all the players. Mary was asked to do something no one had ever done before and no one will ever do again. Hers was an exceptional, powerful and agonizing part to play. In acknowledging that, we are not detracting from God. We are, in fact, glorifying him and his marvelous plan. As the *Catechism* tells us, "What the Catholic faith believes about Mary is based on what it believes about Christ, and what it teaches about Mary illumines in turn its faith in Christ" (*CCC*, 487).

PRAY FOR US SINNERS

But is praying to Mary an attempt to deify her?

Strictly speaking we do not pray to Mary. More accurately, we pray to God, but because he has given us the gift of the communion of saints, he allows our requests to be heard by the saints in heaven. We may therefore *ask for the intercession* of Mary and other saints as well.

Intercession is an important component of the rosary. This prayer is twofold. First, in every Hail Mary we ask the Blessed Mother to pray for us. Second, we offer the rosary for various intentions.

Prayers of intercession have been around for a long time, at least since Abraham's plea on behalf of the righteous few in Sodom (see Genesis 18:22–33). Intercessory prayer is a poignant expression of Christian love, a strengthening of the communion of saints (see *CCC*, 2635). And just as Abraham prayed and pleaded for the many as well as for the one righteous man, the rosary, too, is a prayer for the individual, the family and the world.

The importance of the rosary as intercessory prayer for ourselves and others cannot be underestimated. Ask any Catholic who regularly prays the rosary if he's ever seen results from Mary's intercession, and the answer is sure to be yes. Anecdotes of answered prayer and everyday miracles abound.

Pope John Paul II noted that in our contemporary culture, with its hostility toward the traditional family, the rosary is needed as a means of intercession both *within* and *for* the family. Families who pray together strengthen their bonds and their faith. Offering the rosary for the preservation of the family is a vital contribution to God's kingdom, helping to preserve this building block of society, a foundation created by God.

And the rosary is a powerful intercessory prayer for the world. Pope Benedict XVI has pointed out that in various apparitions Mary has requested that the faithful pray the rosary for peace in the world.[1] Pope John Paul II and many of his predecessors asked the same. John Paul pointed out that a prayer about Jesus, such as the rosary, is "by its nature a prayer for peace" since Jesus is "the Prince of Peace."[2]

The rosary, then, isn't for private devotion only, though it is invaluable as such. It is so much more: Prayed fervently and often, it can enkindle in us the desire for the sanctification and salvation of all mankind, while giving us the means and the form for such intercession.

GOD'S WORK

But what of the Scripture, "For there is one God and there is one mediator between God and men, the man Christ Jesus" (1 Timothy 2:5)?

It is unequivocally true that there is only one mediator for our salvation, "who gave himself as a ransom for all" (1 Timothy 2:6). No one else can reconcile us to the Father; that was and remains the job of Jesus. But this Scripture does not forbid intercessory prayer. As a matter of fact, 1 Timothy 2 begins with "First of all, then, I urge that supplications, prayers, intercessions, and thanksgivings be made for all men" (1 Timothy 2:1).

When we say that Mary intercedes for us, we don't mean that we expect her to *save* us. We mean only that we can ask for the same prayerful intercession that we regularly ask of friends: "The prayer of a righteous man has great power in its effects" (James 5:16). If a fellow Christian can pray for you without fear of usurping God's place, then certainly the saints in heaven can do the same, with even greater power. The doctrine of the communion of saints, based on charity, assures us that "the merciful love of God and his saints is always [attentive] to our prayers" (*CCC*, 962, quoting Paul VI, *Credo of the People of God*, 30).

So while we do ask the Blessed Mother to pray for our needs, we don't expect her to step in and take over God's work. We do not ask her to be our Savior. We ask for her tender, maternal care, and we acknowledge her preeminent role in human history. We offer this woman of unparalleled holiness her due respect, but we do not deify her.

Finally, it's important to note that when we request prayers from a friend (whether on earth or in heaven), we take nothing away from Jesus but *actually fulfill a command from him*. Scripture tells us to pray for one another. In James 5:16 we are told to "pray for one another, that you may be healed." In Ephesians 6:18–19 Paul tells us, "Pray at all times in the Spirit, with all prayer and supplication. To that end keep alert with all perseverance, making supplication for all the saints and also for me." Family, friends and fellow parishioners pray for us regularly, as we pray for them. The communion of saints in heaven does the same, for we are all one body. Of the saints in heaven, the Church assures us:

> [A]fter they have been received into their heavenly home and are present to the Lord, through Him and with Him and in Him they do not cease to intercede with the Father for us, showing forth the merits which they won on earth through the one Mediator between God and man, serving God in all things and filling up in their flesh those things which are lacking of the sufferings of Christ for His Body which is the Church. Thus by their brotherly interest our weakness is greatly strengthened. (*Lumen Gentium,* 49)

So when I request prayers from a friend, I am acting as a faithful member of the body of Christ. I'm having a conversation, in the context of a Christian relationship, with someone who cares about my salvation. The Hail Mary, too, is a conversation. It is a vital part of a living, breathing relationship with someone who cares.

Let's review what we have discovered about the rosary so far. It is:

- a prescribed set of prayers, prayed in rote fashion
- a stable formula that allows us to focus, freeing our hearts and minds for contemplation
- a source of rich imagery that takes us deeply into Scripture and the life of Christ
- the loving intercession of our Blessed Mother
- a legitimate component of the communion of saints and a conversation with the chosen mother of Jesus
- a sure path to intimacy with Jesus Christ

In other words, while we repeat the Hail Mary, we contemplate the life of Christ, ask Mary to take our intentions to her Son and, in so doing, nurture our relationship with him and with Mary as well. Through the rosary we walk Mary's path and learn from this disciple who "lived with her eyes fixed on Christ, treasuring his every word."[3]

Now let's talk about how to pray the rosary.

chapter six

DON'T WORRY

THE MECHANICS OF THE ROSARY

Pray, hope and don't worry.

—SAINT PIO OF PIETRELCINA (PADRE PIO)

It's time for practicalities.

As you talk with others about how to pray the rosary, you might find that contradictions arise about "how it's really prayed":

"I get my rosary done in fifteen minutes flat."

"I spend an hour on my rosary."

"I never say all those extra prayers."

"I say all the introductory prayers, the prayers at the end and the Fatima prayer between each decade."

Who's got it right?

The most important thing to remember is, don't worry about getting it "right." The bare bones of a proper rosary are the decades (an Our Father, ten Hail Marys and the doxology, or Glory Be), a closing Marian prayer (usually Hail, Holy Queen or the Litany of Loreto[1]) and meditating on the mysteries of Christ's life. That's all you have to do to call it a "real" rosary.

Various other prayers, which vary by country and custom, can open and close the rosary. Those other prayers have become an essential part of the rosary for many people, but if you leave out those "extras" you are not praying incorrectly.

Conversely, if you wouldn't dream of omitting those prayers, you are not praying incorrectly either. God hears every version, and they're all valid. There's no standing committee of judges who will grade your performance. Whether you call some of what follows "extra" or "absolutely necessary" is largely a matter of local custom and personal preference and sometimes a matter of private versus public prayer.

The accompanying illustration indicates how people commonly use the beads to count their prayers, but again, you do not have to hold a certain part of the rosary to make it a valid prayer. Fingers work just as well for counting, and so do pages in a book, illustrations of the mysteries, coloring pages for children or whatever you'd like to use. The beads are there to help, not hinder you.

THE BASICS

For the sake of simplicity, I'll use the word *say*, but you may also pray silently. In the explanation that follows, the bold type indicates the part of the prayer to be said by a leader (when the rosary is prayed in a group), and the rest of the prayer is the response.

1. Begin the rosary by making the Sign of the Cross, saying, "In the name of the Father and of the Son and of the Holy Spirit. Amen."

2. Holding the crucifix, say the Apostles' Creed:

   I believe in God, the Father Almighty, Creator of heaven and earth.
   And in Jesus Christ, his only Son, our Lord,
   who was conceived by the Holy Spirit, born of the Virgin Mary,

3rd Mystery:
10 Hail Marys

4th Mystery:
Our Father

3rd Mystery:
Our Father

Glory Be and
Fatima Prayer

Glory Be and
Fatima Prayer

4th Mystery:
10 Hail Marys

2nd Mystery:
10 Hail Marys

5th Mystery:
Our Father

2nd Mystery:
Our Father

Glory Be and
Fatima Prayer

Glory Be and
Fatima Prayer

5th Mystery:
10 Hail Marys

1st Mystery:
10 Hail Marys

1st Mystery:
Our Father

Glory Be and
Fatima Prayer

Glory Be

End with Hail Holy
Queen, Closing
Prayer and Sign of
the Cross

Three Hail Marys for
an increase in faith,
hope and charity

Our Father

Sign of the Cross and
Apostles' Creed

suffered under Pontius Pilate, was crucified, died and
   was buried.

He descended into hell. On the third day he rose again.

He ascended into heaven and is seated at the right hand
   of the Father.

From thence he shall come to judge the living and the dead.

I believe in the Holy Spirit, the holy Catholic Church, the
   communion of saints,

the forgiveness of sins, the resurrection of the body and life ever-
   lasting. Amen.

3. On the first single bead, say an Our Father. Many people offer this Our Father for the intentions of our Holy Father, the pope:

> **Our Father, who art in heaven, hallowed be thy name.**
> **Thy kingdom come, thy will be done, on earth as it is**
> **in heaven.**
> *Give us this day our daily bread, and forgive us our trespasses*
> *as we forgive those who trespass against us.*
> *And lead us not into temptation, but deliver us from evil.*
> *Amen.*

4. On each of the next three beads, say a Hail Mary (these can be offered as prayers for an increase in the virtues of faith, hope and charity in the world):

> **Hail Mary, full of grace, the Lord is with thee.**
> **Blessed art thou among women, and blessed is the fruit**
> **of thy womb, Jesus.**
> *Holy Mary, Mother of God,*
> *pray for us sinners now and at the hour of our death. Amen.*

5. On the next single bead, say a Glory Be:

> **Glory be to the Father and to the Son and to the**
> **Holy Spirit,**
> *as it was in the beginning, is now and ever shall be, world*
> *without end. Amen.*

6. On that same bead you may say what is known as the Fatima Prayer:

> **O my Jesus,** *forgive us our sins. Save us from the fires of hell.*
> *Lead all souls to heaven, especially those in most need of thy*
> *mercy.*

Now you are ready to begin the decades—the ten Hail Marys for each mystery.

1. Remaining on the same bead, announce the first mystery on which you're meditating (and don't get anxious about it!). For example, say, "The first joyful mystery is the Annunciation," or simply think of that mystery. Pray one Our Father and then ten Hail Marys, one for each bead in that set of ten.

2. On the larger bead between decades, say the Glory Be and, if you so choose, the Fatima Prayer. Then say or focus on the second mystery, and pray another Our Father.

3. Pray ten more Hail Marys on the next set of ten beads as you meditate on the second mystery, followed again by a Glory Be and the Fatima Prayer. Continue through the other mysteries in the same way.

4. Many people finish the rosary with the Hail, Holy Queen, also called the *Salve Regina*:

   > ***Hail, holy Queen,*** *mother of mercy, our life, our sweetness and our hope.*
   > *To thee do we cry, poor banished children of Eve.*
   > *To thee do we send up our sighs, mourning and weeping in this valley of tears.*
   > *Turn then, most gracious advocate, thine eyes of mercy toward us,*
   > *and after this our exile show unto us the blessed fruit of thy womb, Jesus.*
   > *O clement, O loving, O sweet Virgin Mary.*
   > ***Pray for us, O holy Mother of God,***
   > *that we may be made worthy of the promises of Christ.*

5. Finish your rosary with the Sign of the Cross: "In the name of the Father, and of the Son and of the Holy Spirit. Amen."

THE EXTRAS

Some people add the following prayer at the end of the rosary, especially when it is prayed in a group; others pray it at the beginning of the rosary:

Let us pray:

O God, whose only begotten Son, by his life, death, and resur-
rection,
has purchased for us the rewards of eternal salvation,
grant, we beseech thee, that while meditating on these mysteries
of the most holy rosary of the Blessed Virgin Mary,
we may both imitate what they contain and obtain what they
promise,
through the same Christ our Lord. Amen.

Another addition might be the Saint Michael Prayer:

Saint Michael the Archangel, *defend us in battle.*
Be our protection against the wickedness and snares of the
devil.
May God rebuke him, we humbly pray, and do thou,
O Prince of the heavenly host, by the power of God,
cast into hell Satan and all the evil spirits
who prowl about the world seeking the ruin of souls. Amen.

Finally a leader might add, "For the intentions of the Holy Father," and then pray one more Our Father, Hail Mary and Glory Be.

Again, after whatever prayers you have included, finish your rosary with the Sign of the Cross: "In the name of the Father and of the Son and of the Holy Spirit. Amen."

Some people feel strongly about including all of the accompanying prayers. Depending on custom or tradition in your area, there may be more or less than what's listed here. There is certainly much spiritual value in these additions, as there is in any prayer. They can enhance your rosary with their "added fruit."

But others might feel equally strongly that the inclusion of extra prayers is unnecessary for their rosary routine. Perhaps they grew up without these extras as part of the family rosary and never learned them. Perhaps they feel that too many additions add a burdensome time constraint.

Whatever the reasons, we needn't debate the issue. Both views are legitimate. We may each pray the rosary as best suits us. Variations on a rosary are not a matter of doctrine but a matter of habit, taste, training or preference. Do what works best for you, and rest in the knowledge that all "versions" of the prayer are valid, and both are hastened by Our Lady to the throne of God.

Now that we have the mechanics down, we'll do our best to keep the prayer from becoming mechanical. It's time to incorporate the mysteries, which raise the prayer from a simple recitation to a transcendent and profound conversation with God.

chapter seven

"*L*EARNING *H*IM"

THE MYSTERIES OF THE ROSARY

Christ is the supreme Teacher, the revealer and the one revealed. It is not just a question of learning what he taught but of *"learning him."*

—POPE JOHN PAUL II, *Rosarium Virginis Mariae,* 14

One cannot talk for long about the rosary without addressing the mysteries. They are the meat of the rosary that feeds and sustains us. Without the mysteries to enrich them, our prayers are in danger of becoming superstitious repetition.

That's not to say we're all called to meditate at the level of mystics such as Saint John of the Cross and Saint Teresa of Avila. It is important, however, to understand the role of the mysteries and their value in drawing us closer to Jesus. But before we proceed any further, it might be helpful to define what is meant by *mystery.*

A MYSTERY TO ME

I have to confess that before I became a Christian, I thought Christians used the word *mystery* with alarming frequency. It seemed an all-too convenient dodge. Unable to comprehend the

Trinity? That's OK, it's a mystery. Don't know how to explain the virgin birth? Another mystery. How can we believe that God could become man? Welcome to the mystery club. It was *all* a mystery, or so it seemed to the skeptic in me.

It wasn't until I became a Catholic that someone adequately explained the term *mystery* in its theological context. A mystery doesn't simply mean "We don't get it." A mystery is a truth of the faith that we know only because God has *revealed* it to us. It is a mystery precisely because it is not a conclusion we can reach on our own, without God's intervention and revelation. In other words, it's not the obvious, "reasonable" answer.

But that doesn't mean we've checked our minds at the door. It does mean that, thanks to divine revelation, we know something we would otherwise not know. That something is indeed "a mystery" in the theological sense: It must be accepted on faith, because even after such revelation, we cannot fully grasp its truth. That's not a dodge. It's a fact.

The mysteries of the lives of Jesus and Mary, then, are truths of the faith revealed to us by God and preserved for us in Scripture and Sacred Tradition. They are the truths on which we meditate when we pray the rosary.

From our brief look at the history of the rosary, we know that for about five hundred years, there were three sets of Mysteries: the Joyful, the Sorrowful and the Glorious. In 2002 Pope John Paul II did something no one had done for a very long time: He added something new to the rosary, making new history.

Remember, praying the rosary a particular way is not a matter of doctrine. The history of the rosary shows us that it has been refined over the years. John Paul II found the time ripe for a little more refinement.

In his apostolic letter *Rosarium Virginis Mariae* ("The Rosary of the Blessed Virgin Mary"), the Holy Father proclaimed

October 2002 through October 2003 the Year of the Rosary. And he added to the rosary the Mysteries of Light or, as they are often called, the Luminous Mysteries. Today, then, we have four sets of mysteries, twenty mysteries in all, on which to meditate.

What follows is a complete list of the mysteries and some corresponding Scripture references. There are a number of Scriptures that could be cited for each mystery, and in various books and other aids to prayer, you'll find a variety of choices. For example, cited below for the first mystery (the Annunciation) is Luke 1:26–27, but the encounter between the angel Gabriel and Mary continues for several more verses. And some mysteries of the rosary can be found in more than one Gospel.

The Scripture references here then are a starting point. For the sake of simplicity and consistency with Rome, I have included the passages referenced by the Vatican on its Web site (www.vatican.va) along with the Vatican's corresponding references from the *Catechism of the Catholic Church*.

I've also noted the days on which each set of mysteries is traditionally prayed. Pope John Paul II, in *Rosarium Virginis Mariae*, pointed out that such guidelines are not intended to limit our freedom. The suggested cycle of prayer offers structure, as do liturgy and the structure of the rosary itself. By rotating through the various mysteries during the week, we journey regularly "through the mysteries of the life of Christ."[1]

That's not to say we can't vary the way we pray. I have found that at certain times in my life, I've focused more on one set of mysteries than another, according to my circumstances. During Lent or during a time of mourning or suffering, for example, I may pray only the Sorrowful Mysteries and find great comfort in them. When I was last expecting a baby, I focused on the Joyful Mysteries. The suggested days, then, are just that: ideas that can be helpful but certainly not requirements.

THE JOYFUL MYSTERIES

These mysteries are called "joyful" because they flow from the great joy that is the Incarnation.[2] They are commonly prayed on Mondays and Saturdays.

1. THE ANNUNCIATION

In the sixth month the angel Gabriel was sent from God to a city of Galilee named Nazareth, to a virgin betrothed to a man whose name was Joseph, of the house of David; and the virgin's name was Mary. (Luke 1:26–27)

The Annunciation to Mary inaugurates the "fullness of time" [Galatians 4:4], the time of the fulfilment of God's promises and preparations. (*CCC*, 484)

2. THE VISITATION

In those days Mary arose and went with haste into the hill country, to a city of Judah, and she entered the house of Zechariah and greeted Elizabeth. And when Elizabeth heard the greeting of Mary, the child leaped in her womb; and Elizabeth was filled with the Holy Spirit and she exclaimed with a loud cry, "Blessed are you among women, and blessed is the fruit of your womb!" (Luke 1:39–42)

Mary's visitation to Elizabeth thus became a visit from God to his people. (*CCC*, 717)

3. THE BIRTH OF OUR LORD

In those days a decree went out from Caesar Augustus that all the world should be enrolled. This was the first enrolment, when Quirinius was governor of Syria. And all went to be enrolled, each to his own city. And Joseph also went up from Galilee, from the city of Nazareth, to Judea, to the city of David, which is called Bethlehem, because he was of the house and lineage of David, to be enrolled with Mary his betrothed, who was with child. And while they were there, the time came for her to be delivered. And she gave birth to her first-born son and wrapped him in swaddling cloths, and laid him in a manger, because there was no place for them in the inn. (Luke 2:1–7)

Jesus was born in a humble stable, into a poor family. Simple shepherds were the first witnesses to this event. In this poverty heaven's glory was made manifest. (*CCC*, 525)

4. THE PRESENTATION OF THE CHILD JESUS IN THE TEMPLE
And at the end of eight days, when he was circumcised, he was called Jesus, the name given by the angel before he was conceived in the womb.

And when the time came for their purification according to the law of Moses, they brought him up to Jerusalem to present him to the Lord (as it is written in the law of the Lord, "Every male that opens the womb shall be called holy to the Lord") and to offer a sacrifice according to what is said in the law of the Lord, "a pair of turtledoves, or two young pigeons." (Luke 2:21–24)

Jesus' *circumcision,* on the eighth day after his birth, is the sign of his incorporation into Abraham's descendants, into the people of the covenant. It is the sign of his submission to the Law. (*CCC,* 527)

5. THE FINDING OF JESUS IN THE TEMPLE

Now his parents went to Jerusalem every year at the feast of the Passover. And when he was twelve years old, they went up according to custom; and when the feast was ended, as they were returning, the boy Jesus stayed behind in Jerusalem. His parents did not know it.... After three days they found him in the temple, sitting among the teachers, listening to them and asking them questions; and all who heard him were amazed at his understanding and his answers. (Luke 2:41–43, 46–47)

The *finding of Jesus in the temple* is the only event that breaks the silence of the Gospels about the hidden years of Jesus. Here Jesus lets us catch a glimpse of the mystery of his total consecration to a mission that flows from his divine sonship: "Did you not know that I must be about my Father's work?" [Luke 2:49]. (*CCC*, 534)

THE LUMINOUS MYSTERIES

The Mysteries of Light are so called because they are *revelations "of the Kingdom now present in the very person of Jesus."*[3] Through these events Jesus reveals who he is and what he has come to do. Pope John Paul II suggested that these mysteries be prayed on Thursdays.

1. THE BAPTISM OF JESUS

And when Jesus was baptized, he went up immediately from the water, and behold, the heavens were opened and he saw the Spirit of God descending like a dove, and alighting on him; and behold, a voice from heaven, saying, "This is my beloved Son, with whom I am well pleased." (Matthew 3:16–17)

Jesus' public life begins with his baptism by John in the Jordan [see Luke 3:23; Acts 1:22]. John preaches "a baptism of repentance for the forgiveness of sins" [Luke 3:3]. (*CCC*, 535)

2. THE WEDDING FEAST AT CANA

On the third day there was a marriage at Cana in Galilee, and the mother of Jesus was there; Jesus also was invited to the marriage, with his disciples. When the wine failed, the mother of Jesus said to him, "They have no wine." And Jesus said to her, "O woman, what have you to do with me? My hour has not yet come." His mother said to the servants, "Do whatever he tells you." (John 2:1–5)

On the threshold of his public life Jesus performs his first sign—at his mother's request—during a wedding feast: The Church attaches great importance to Jesus' presence at the wedding at Cana. She sees in it the confirmation of the goodness of marriage and the proclamation that thenceforth marriage will be an efficacious sign of Christ's presence. (*CCC*, 1613)

3. THE PROCLAMATION OF THE KINGDOM OF GOD

"The time is fulfilled, and the kingdom of God is at hand; repent, and believe in the gospel." (Mark 1:15)

Everyone is called to enter the Kingdom. First announced to the children of Israel, this messianic kingdom is intended to accept men of all nations [see Matthew 8:11; 10;5–7; 28:19]. (*CCC*, 543)

4. THE TRANSFIGURATION

And after six days Jesus took with him Peter and James and John his brother, and led them up a high mountain apart. And he was transfigured before them, and his face shone like the sun, and his garments became white as light. (Matthew 17:1–2)

For a moment Jesus discloses his divine glory, confirming Peter's confession. He also reveals that he will have to go by the way of the cross at Jerusalem in order to "enter into his glory" [Luke 24:26]. (*CCC,* 555)

5. THE INSTITUTION OF THE EUCHARIST

Now as they were eating, Jesus took bread, and blessed, and broke it, and gave it to the disciples and said, "Take, eat; this is my body" (Matthew 26:26).

By celebrating the Last Supper with his apostles in the course of the Passover meal, Jesus gave the Jewish Passover its definitive meaning. Jesus' passing over to his father by his death and Resurrection, the new Passover, is anticipated in the Supper and celebrated in the Eucharist, which fulfills the Jewish Passover and anticipates the final Passover of the Church in the glory of the kingdom. (*CCC,* 1340)

THE SORROWFUL MYSTERIES

The Sorrowful Mysteries recount the passion and death of Jesus. They are traditionally prayed on Tuesdays and Fridays.

1. THE AGONY IN THE GARDEN

Then Jesus went with them to a place called Gethsemane, and he said to his disciples, "Sit here, while I go over there and pray." And taking with him Peter and the two sons of Zebedee, he began to be sorrowful and troubled. Then he said to them, "My soul is very sorrowful, even to death; remain here, and watch with me." And going a little farther he fell on his face and prayed, "My Father, if it be possible, let this chalice pass from me; nevertheless, not as I will, but as thou will." (Matthew 26:36–39)

Such a battle and such a victory become possible only through prayer. It is by his prayer that Jesus vanquishes the tempter, both at the outset of his public mission and in the ultimate struggle of his agony [see Matthew 4:1–11; 26:36–44]. (*CCC,* 2849)

2. THE SCOURGING AT THE PILLAR

Then Pilate took Jesus and scourged him. And the soldiers plaited a crown of thorns, and put it on his head, and clothed him in a purple robe; they came up to him, saying, "Hail, King of the Jews!" and struck him with their hands. (John 19:1–3)

Jesus' sufferings took their historical, concrete form from the fact that he was "rejected by the elders and the chief priests and the scribes" (Mk 8:31), who "handed him to the Gentiles to be mocked and scourged and crucified" (Mt 20:19). (*CCC,* 572)

3. THE CROWNING WITH THORNS

Then the soldiers of the governor took Jesus into the praetorium, and they gathered the whole battalion before him. And they stripped him and put a scarlet robe upon him, and plaiting a crown of thorns they put it on his head, and put a reed in his right hand. And kneeling before him they mocked him, saying, "Hail, King of the Jews!" (Matthew 27:27–29)

It is love "to the end" [John 13:1] that confers on Christ's sacrifice its value as redemption and reparation, as atonement and satisfaction. He knew and loved us all when he offered his life [see Galatians 2:20; Ephesians 5:2, 25]. (*CCC*, 616)

4. THE CARRYING OF THE CROSS

And they compelled a passer-by, Simon of Cyrene, who was coming in from the country, the father of Alexander and Rufus, to carry his cross. And they brought him to the place called Golgotha (which means the place of a skull). (Mark 15:21–22)

By accepting in his human will that the Father's will be done, he accepts his death as redemptive, for "he himself bore our sins in his body on the tree" [1 Peter 2:24; see Matthew 26:42]. (*CCC*, 612)

5. THE CRUCIFIXION

And when they came to the place which is called The Skull, there they crucified him, and the criminals, one on the right and one on the left. And Jesus said, "Father, forgive them; for they know not what they do."

…

It was now about the sixth hour, and there was darkness over the whole land until the ninth hour, while the sun's light failed; and the curtain of the temple was torn in two. Then Jesus, crying with a loud voice, said, "Father, into your hands I commit my spirit!" And having said this he breathed his last. (Luke 23:33–34, 44–46)

"Christ died for our sins in accordance with the scriptures" [1 Corinthians 15:3]. (*CCC*, 619)

THE GLORIOUS MYSTERIES

Christ's life certainly didn't end with the crucifixion. The Glorious Mysteries take us through his Resurrection and beyond. These are traditionally prayed on Wednesday and on the day of Resurrection, Sunday.

1. THE RESURRECTION

But on the first day of the week, at early dawn, they went to the tomb, taking the spices which they had prepared. And they found the stone rolled away from the tomb, but when they went in they did not find the body. While they were perplexed about this, behold, two men stood by them in dazzling apparel; and as they were frightened and bowed their faces to the ground, the men said to them, "Why do you seek the living among the dead? He is not here, but has risen." (Luke 24:1–5)

"If Christ has not been raised, then our preaching is in vain and your faith is in vain" [1 Corinthians 15:14]. The Resurrection above all constitutes the confirmation of all Christ's works and teachings. (*CCC*, 651)

2. THE ASCENSION

So then the Lord Jesus, after he had spoken to them, was taken up into heaven, and sat down at the right hand of God. (Mark 16:19)

THE ROSARY

This final stage stays closely linked to the first, that is, to his descent from heaven in the Incarnation. Only the one who "came from the Father" can return to the Father: Christ Jesus [see John 16:28]. (*CCC*, 661)

3. THE DESCENT OF THE HOLY SPIRIT

When the day of Pentecost had come, they were all together in one place. And suddenly a sound came from heaven like the rush of a mighty wind, and it filled all the house where they were sitting. And there appeared to them tongues as of fire, distributed and resting on each one of them. And they were all filled with the Holy Spirit and began to speak in other tongues, as the Spirit gave them utterance. (Acts 2:1–4)

"Holy Spirit" is the proper name of the one whom we adore and glorify with the Father and the Son. The Church has received this name from the Lord and professes it in the Baptism of her new children [see Matthew 28:19]. (*CCC*, 691)

4. THE ASSUMPTION

Henceforth all generations will call me blessed; for he who is mighty has done great things for me. (Luke 1:48–49)

The Most Blessed Virgin Mary, when the course of her earthly life was completed, was taken up body and soul into the glory of heaven, where she already shares in the glory of her Son's Resurrection, anticipating the resurrection of all members of his Body. (*CCC*, 974)

5. THE CROWNING OF OUR LADY QUEEN OF HEAVEN

And a great sign appeared in heaven, a woman clothed with the sun, with the moon under her feet, and on her head a crown of twelve stars. (Revelation 12:1)

"Finally the Immaculate Virgin, preserved free from all stain of original sin, when the course of her earthly life was finished, was taken up body and soul into heavenly glory, and exalted by the Lord as Queen over all things, so that she might be the more fully conformed to her Son, the Lord of lords and conqueror of sin and death [*Lumen Gentium,* 59; see Pius XII, *Munificentissimus Deus* (1950): DS 3903; see Revelation 19:16]." (*CCC,* 966)

Now that you're familiar with the mysteries, you might ask, "What do I do with them?" How do we pray the mysteries and experience fruitful meditation? That's the subject of the next chapter.

chapter eight

UNFATHOMABLE RICHES

MEDITATING ON THE MYSTERIES

By its nature the recitation of the rosary calls for a quiet rhythm and a lingering pace, helping the individual to meditate on the mysteries of the Lord's life as seen through the eyes of her who was closest to the Lord. In this way the unfathomable riches of these mysteries are unfolded.

—POPE PAUL VI, *Marialis Cultus,* 47

In chapter three I mentioned that meditation is "a quest" (*CCC,* 2705) for greater understanding of God and our life with him. This quest uses "thought, imagination, emotion, and desire" (*CCC,* 2708) to whet our appetites for a more meaningful relationship with Jesus Christ. That is its purpose.

We don't meditate in order to pass a prayer test or be able to chat with friends about how fascinating meditation is. We do it as a means to an end: to grow closer to Jesus. Regularly employed, meditation *will* do that. Let's see how it works.

We're after "thought, imagination, emotion and desire." Substitute one of those words for *meditation,* and see what happens.

Instead of "*Meditate* on the third joyful mystery," try "*Think* about the birth of Jesus." Now try the other elements of meditation too: "*Imagine* what it was like to witness the birth of Jesus. What *emotions* did Mary feel at his birth? What about Joseph? The shepherds? How would *I* have felt if I'd been there? Do I *desire* to be transformed by the birth of Jesus? What do I desire?"

When we substitute these simple words, suddenly meditation isn't so intimidating. It is not some sort of dreamy, otherworldly condition or altered state of consciousness. It does not necessarily involve something dramatic, like weeping or levitating. Meditation is simply focusing on God or, more specifically, focusing on one thing about God at a time. And in breaking down our thoughts about God to one piece of his life at a time—one episode, one teaching or one demonstration of his love—we are "learning him."

This "one thing at a time" concept is an important one. Our minds are in constant motion—planning, thinking, plotting and wandering. Meditation is a way of herding the stray thoughts, corralling them and setting them aside for a time, so that we have room for the moment's "one thing."

Don't expect this to go well immediately, and don't worry if it doesn't. Even with time and practice you can expect to fail on a regular basis. Seasoned rosary prayers and meditation experts of all stripes can tell same stories: minds that slip away to the pattering of rain on the roof, to the growling of a stomach or the creaking of a knee, to the concern over a prickly client or that slow but determined student. Then there's the newborn baby, the weeping adolescent in need of attention or the incessant ringing of the phone. All of these things will conspire against you as you try to enter into meaningful meditation.

But don't be fooled into thinking these distractions and interruptions mean you should give up. Instead, realize that you're just another fallen human being and you've done what God knew you would do: You've fallen down. All you have to do is get up again. And again. And, yes, again.

That's an enormous part of our role in this drama: determination and perseverance. As long as we persist in *trying* to imagine, think about, feel and desire God, we're doing our work. *We* can't conjure a powerful prayer experience; God is in charge of that. But we can make ourselves available for one. And if we do, he'll sometimes drop in on our prayer time in unexpected ways. We might feel a powerful sense of comfort, a new dose of strength and fortitude, or simply that we've rested in his presence and now have the courage to face a tough situation. Those are the times we can cling to, revisit, hope for and build on as our prayer lives grow and flourish.

But other times we'll come away as dry as a Judean desert, ready to berate ourselves for thinking of nothing but pizza during prayer. When that happens it can be helpful to spend a little time considering the simple but profound truth that God is our Father.

The image of a father is not a random one; God chose it deliberately. Granted, our perceptions of God as Father can be tainted by difficult or even painful earthly associations with that relationship. But remember that God is the *ideal* Father. We should measure earthly fathers by the godly ideal, rather than measuring God by the fallen, earthly examples we may have encountered. God our Father takes care of us in the same way that an earthly father should love, protect, shelter and provide for his family.

Can you imagine an earthly father getting angry with a five-year-old who repeatedly falls down while trying to master a two-wheeler? No, a good father watches his child's brave efforts, sabotaged as they are by youth and immaturity, with pride and overflowing affection. He marvels at his child's perseverance and desire to please.

I like to imagine God the Father watching us in much the same way. He knows how limited we are, how utterly lacking in all that's necessary for spiritual perfection. Nevertheless he is full of affection for our fumbling ways, our determination and our desire to please. And like the father who will cheer wildly when the two-wheeler is conquered, jumping up and down and waving to the child who's now gliding down the street, God our Father will cheer us on with consolations and encouragement as we grow closer to him in prayer.

So don't worry about the fumbling and the falls. Push on and keep trying.

PRAYING THE MYSTERIES

Now that we know what the mysteries are and that meditation means "think, imagine, feel and desire the things of God," let's take a look at how that actually plays out. When you sit down to pray a rosary (or kneel, though it's perfectly fine to stand, lie in bed, walk, run or do whatever you want to do while you pray), it might look like this:

You want to pray the Joyful Mysteries. You think about the Annunciation, the angel Gabriel's announcement to Mary that she's been chosen to be the mother of our Lord. As you begin an Our Father and ten Hail Marys, focus your thoughts only on that scene. Perhaps you wonder what it would feel like to have an angel appear before you. Would you be terrified? Would you doubt, faint or scoff? What did Mary think?

Or you might focus on the fact that Mary said yes to God. This gets you thinking about the ways in which *you* respond to God every day. Are you saying yes, or are you holding back? In what ways are you not giving yourself completely to him? This leads you to pray that he'll help you say yes to everything he asks of you.

You have just meditated.

Here's another example: When you pray the Sorrowful Mysteries, you might "place" yourself in a scene. Where are you during the Crucifixion? Are you hiding, or are you standing at the foot of the cross? Are you ashamed to know Jesus, or are you courageous? Is what you imagine yourself doing what you're really doing today? How have you denied Jesus, and how have you stood up for him?

During one Lent I spent some extended time every day contemplating the Sorrowful Mysteries, placing myself directly in each scene. I imagined how it must have felt to be there—what Mary Magdalene said and felt, what the Blessed Mother endured. I contemplated my sins—those actual sins for which Jesus died—and how those sins contributed to his agony. The results were profoundly moving, and I still remember that year as one the most fruitful Lents I've ever experienced.

As thoughts and feelings about the mysteries run through your mind, you're simultaneously praying Hail Marys. That's when the physical aid of the rosary beads comes into play. You don't have to worry about counting, because your fingers will let you know when you've reached the end of a decade. When you finish one, you move on to the next and shift your thoughts to the next mystery.

"But," you may ask, "what if I get so caught up in a particular meditation that I stop saying Hail Marys? What if I spend fifteen minutes contemplating the ways I need to say yes to God and suddenly realize that my prayer time is over?" You have to shower and get to work, and you haven't finished your whole rosary!

Well, congratulations. You have just spent fifteen minutes in fruitful prayer. Consider it the end of your morning rosary and the beginning of a flourishing prayer life.

Remember, it's not about chalking up the right number of Hail Marys, despite the fact that the structure of the prayer and the counting *are* helpful. It's about communicating with God.

PERSEVERANCE PAYS

On the other hand, you might drone through fifteen minutes of Hail Marys and experience no "real" meditation. Yes, your lips were moving, but you forgot entirely about the Luminous Mysteries, and you couldn't ignore the smell of coffee.

Believe it or not, it's OK. You have just given fifteen minutes to God. You had a lesson on that two-wheeler and you fell down. And tomorrow you'll try again.

A friend of mine once shared her temptation to stop praying the rosary because it had become dry and mechanical. She was merely going through the motions and wondered what the point was.

We talked about the fact that prayers are sacramentals. Remember that sacramentals, including prayers, are sacred symbols that dispose us to receive grace. Simple *words* are transformed when they are used in the service of God and therefore can have a transforming effect on us, even when we aren't feeling the effect. The words of a prayer are valuable, in and of themselves, because God allows them to be so. Even mechanical praying is a more valuable way of spending fifteen minutes than not praying. Simply repeating the holy name of Jesus, for example, has great power.

I encouraged my friend to keep praying even when it felt bone-dry. To pray is better than not to pray, and even the time we spend in dry prayer can be beneficial. It can strengthen habit, discipline and commitment and can carry us through the desert until we find the next oasis of consolation. So the rosary can serve as a helpful vehicle during dry times.

It's important to keep in mind that prayer is not about feeling good. At times our prayer will feel sublime, but sometimes after prayer we won't feel consoled or happy at all. We'll think our prayer time was neither fruitful nor deep nor meaningful. But if we give up praying during the dry, tough times and wait until we "feel like it" again, that time may never come. On the other hand, if we keep our appointments with God, continuing to pray during the desolation, we will be available to him when he next drops an unexpected gift in our hands. And sometimes the most powerful prayer will happen when you least expect it.

Several years ago I was in the hospital, recovering from a procedure following a miscarriage. I remember praying the rosary as I struggled to come out of the anesthesia. I murmured a few Hail Marys, drifted away, prayed a few more and sank back into sleep. By all outward accounts it couldn't have *looked* like fruitful prayer time. But I remember how powerfully connected to Mary I felt.

I was offering those prayers for my husband, who was still, by his own admission, stubbornly outside the Catholic faith. I asked Mary to pray for me, that I could peacefully accept God's will for the baby we'd just lost, and I offered my suffering for Tom's conversion. My prayers were mumbled and hazy, but the meditation in my heart was clear.

Miraculously, within a couple months, my husband made the decision to be received into the Catholic Church. Mary had gathered up my pain and my plea and gently deposited them at the Lord's feet, and he graciously answered my prayers. The Blessed Mother *always* leads us to her Son.

We may think that the ideal rosary is the one we plan, the one during which we take our time, move at a leisurely pace and experience meditations that are rich and transformative. But the less-than-ideal rosaries are still precious times spent in prayer and can be just as powerful. We all yearn for quality *and* quantity, and sometimes we get both. But sometimes we get neither. Just push on. Don't give up if your quality crumbles. It will return, in God's time.

And in the meantime, you are learning him.

chapter nine

MAKING IT WORK

And he told them a parable, to the effect that they ought always
to pray and not lose heart.

—LUKE 18:1

Now that we've explored every other aspect of the rosary, let's ask
the real question: How do we put this into action for more than
a week? It's a question every serious Christian faces, no matter
what the form of prayer is.

It's the question of a realist. We have the noblest intentions.
We *mean* to go to God every day, to give ourselves to him twenty-
four hours a day, seven days a week. But we routinely fall down
on the job. How then do we make it happen for real?

GOD'S PART

First know this: Prayer is hard. It comforts me to know there's a
sizable section in the *Catechism of the Catholic Church* called "The
Battle of Prayer" (see *CCC*, 2725–2745). There we are reminded
that although we are battling "against ourselves and against the
wiles of the tempter who does all he can to turn man away from
prayer, away from union with God" (*CCC*, 2725), we are not
alone in this battle. God can and does arm us for the fight.

I also find it consoling to pick up the Bible and read about the Old Testament patriarchs. They weren't always a whole lot better at this stuff than we are. (As you read Scripture, be on the lookout for kindred spirits. You'll find a number of them.)

Consider Moses, for example. In Exodus, chapter three, God initiates prayer (a conversation) with him. Moses starts off admirably, responding, "Here am I" (Exodus 3:4). So far, so good. But when God assigns Moses his first important task, Moses starts in with the arguments.

First he wants to know how he'll prove to the Israelites that he *really* talked to the Lord. God explains to Moses exactly how he'll make his case, patiently redirecting Moses to the task at hand.

But then Moses protests that he's not an eloquent speaker, and he'll be terrible at this assignment. God counters calmly, as God will, with his utter support, again patiently explaining that Moses will be given the right words at the right time, as well as the courage to say them. But what does Moses do next, now that God has provided for all his needs?

He has another less-than-stellar moment. He basically whines, "Couldn't you just get somebody else for the job?" But God, being God, wants the man he has chosen. God wins. Moses finally is convinced and is willing and determined to do his part.

Does this sound familiar?

We'd all *like* to leap immediately to being willing and determined, but most of us are a lot like Moses. It takes time and some persistence on God's part before we warm up to his plans and accept what he has called us to do.

As we saw in the exchange with Moses, God is the one who initiates the contact. He begins prayer, which is a "gift of grace" for us (*CCC*, 2725). But after God initiates it, we have a responsibility. We have to respond. We might fight him or try to argue our way out of his plan or deny that we're the best one for the job. We may feel inadequate or wonder how his plan will ever work out. But God is good. He will provide for all we need, just as he did for Moses.

Romans 8:26 tells us that "the Spirit helps us in our weakness; for we do not know how to pray as we ought, but the Spirit himself intercedes for us with sighs too deep for words." Prayer then is not a purely human endeavor. We "do not know how to pray," but there *is* help, and it comes from the Holy Spirit. That's a necessary and heartening reminder when we're putting together our battle plan for prayer.

OUR PART

Like anything worth doing, prayer takes commitment, practice and discipline, which means we can't simply wait for it to happen. Once God has called us, we have to actively do our part. And as baptized Christians, we know he's already begun his work in us. It's time for us to respond. We may need to develop a few new habits. Then, in time, it *will* "just happen." But not at first.

Consider your habits. We've all tried to change undesirable ones: smoking, eating ice cream every night, a sedentary life or yelling at the kids. And when we want to abandon old habits, we begin to examine how to tackle certain situations more constructively. We look at alternatives: Take a walk instead of having a cigarette, eat something healthy instead of that mile-high bowl of Rocky Road, ride a bike to work, count to ten before speaking. And once we consider some practical substitutions, we make preparations: Throw out the cigarettes, toss away the ice cream, check the tires on the bike and hug the kids. Then we implement the plan.

The same is true for prayer. If we want to see progress, we need to examine our habits, set a few goals and start the preparations. A little bit of planning can go a long way toward real change, and that includes our prayer lives.

First, consider where you might find fifteen or twenty minutes in your day. That's all it takes to start. As your commitment to the rosary grows, the time you spend with it may increase, but not necessarily. A fruitful rosary can happen in a fairly short amount of time, so start with fifteen or twenty minutes. Here are a few ideas:

- Get up fifteen minutes earlier than usual. Get out for a walk first thing in the morning, and pray as you walk.
- Use fifteen minutes of your lunch break for prayer.
- Are you at home with babies or small children? Pray during nap time.
- Are you at home with older children? Enforce "quiet time" after lunch, and pray then.
- Any time before dinner to grab fifteen minutes? A window of opportunity after?
- Give up one TV show in the evening. Replace it with prayer time.
- Get ready for bed a little earlier, and pray for fifteen minutes before you go to sleep.
- Do you usually read before sleep? Slip a rosary into your reading-in-bed time.
- Stay up fifteen minutes later than usual.

I can already hear the objections. (Remember Moses?) "Sure, that works for you, but my kids won't nap." "I already get up at five AM. I can't get up any earlier."

In certain seasons of life, it seems that even if we really dig, even when we think there *might* be one or two places to carve out a few extra minutes, we realize we were wrong. There's simply no time, and it just doesn't seem possible after all. So we go back to God and say, "Can't you just get somebody else?"

But God has a few more ideas for us, just as he did for Moses. He knows that our lives are so busy and full that sometimes we really *don't* have time for anything outside of what we're already doing. Maybe you're working three jobs to support your family. Perhaps you're the mother of ten children, or you're a student who's working or studying every waking moment. You can honestly say that you rise at a ridiculous hour, stay up too late in the pursuit of your vocation, fall asleep the minute you even think of the word *pillow* and cannot imagine how to find another fifteen-minute chunk in your day without its killing you.

Relax. God understands. Life *is* busy, and it is hard to find time. For many of us our time has already been found and claimed by others.

But God has an answer for every objection we raise, just as he did for Moses. He will equip us, whether we like it or not. Even when we're occupied every waking hour, we can still pray.

Finding Time

Prayer can be woven into things we're already doing. Here are a few ideas to get you started with that approach:

- Pray in the shower. (Yes, your level of meditation will be affected, but give it a try. You have to shower anyway, right?)
- Do you run, use a treadmill or go to a gym? Try praying the rosary while you work out. The rosary may not have a great pounding beat, but it has its own kind of rhythm. You can even download a version of it onto your MP3 player.
- Do you commute to work? Pray in the car. (Yes, your level of meditation will be affected. Do *not* contemplate the

mysteries so deeply that you have an accident. But remember, praying anywhere is better than not praying at all.)

- Gather your napless children together and pray a rosary or even a decade with them. (Yes, your level of meditation will be affected, but your sweet children just might stun you with their innocent insights.)
- Find a Catholic TV or radio station that broadcasts the rosary and pray along if the broadcast time meshes with your routine.
- Buy a CD of the rosary (or use the version you downloaded for workouts), and pray while working around the house. You can pray while washing dishes, doing laundry, tackling home repairs, changing the oil, scrubbing the toilet, pushing the lawnmower, changing a diaper or cleaning the gutters.
- Pray while you make breakfast, lunch or dinner.
- Pray while you do something dull and mindless at work. (If your work is never dull and mindless, then thank God for that gift.)
- Pray while you walk the floor at 4 AM with a sick or fussy baby. Or pray while you rock and nurse, and rock and nurse, and rock and nurse…
- Pray as you snuggle next to your spouse while he watches TV. (Yes, your level of meditation will be affected.) Plug into a recording of the rosary or some music; classical and chant can be great aids to prayer. Thank your spouse for understanding, and be sure to pray for him.
- Or excuse yourself for the first fifteen minutes of a show, promising you'll be back soon. Better yet, turn off the TV and pray together.

You get the idea. We can pray while doing all sorts of things. I hear you asking, however, "Do those times *count*?"

Remember that *everything* counts. It is better to pray than not to pray. And while it's true that some prayer times will feel more meaningful than others, it's not about how we feel; it's about praying. And as you experiment you'll begin to discover the times that are (or have the potential to be) most fruitful for you.

Persevering and praying through the busy days and seasons of life will keep you in touch with the Lord. If you put prayer off until the day you have "enough time," you may find that you no longer know the God you want to pray to. Don't lose touch with him just because life is busy.

So begin where you are, with the life you've been given. Work with the schedule you have, then work to make it better.

Few schedules are perfect, but there's a hidden benefit in that fact. The imperfections make us hungry for more and better prayer. Our experiments and even our failures make us more adept seekers of the elusive fifteen minutes. Eventually what was once a less-than-perfect prayer life *will* improve. As new prayer habits become a way of life, we will want "always to pray." And because we *are* praying, we will "not lose heart" (Luke 18:1).

But if we are tempted to lose heart, it's extremely helpful to remember that life changes frequently. We may be too busy right now to easily find fifteen minutes, but that won't always be the case. Students graduate, babies grow up, sleep patterns change, commutes to work vary, schedules shift like sand. What seems impossible today can look quite different two years down the road.

"But I Can't..."

At this point the final protests may rise up. It's the Moses in us. We've argued and fought, and we're still trying to get out of prayer with what sound like valid excuses. But the bottom line is, either we're praying (which really just means talking to God) or we're not. It's up to us.

If you're in the final stages of denial, I hope that something of the following will help you. Take heart, and remember Moses. The Lord will provide.

- "But I can't use my lunch break. I have to eat." It's OK to pray and eat at the same time.
- "But I can't pray during the kids' nap time. I have to clean." Try the pray-while-you-clean approach.
- "But I can't give up TV. That's my only real time to unwind." You don't have to give up your entire evening to prayer, just one show or maybe only half of a show. Praying might even revive you in ways you never anticipated.
- "But I can't get up earlier *or* go to bed later." Remember, there are lots of ways to weave prayer into other activities; give one of them a try.
- "But I can't pray at bedtime. I'll fall asleep." We've all said this one; we've all *done* this one. If bedtime is truly the only time you have for prayer, use it. Yes, you may fall asleep, but God will understand. That doesn't mean you should postpone prayer when you know that you'll fade away with the first Our Father. But if you *do* fall asleep during your only *real* free time, you shouldn't fret.
- The rosary is, after all, a very relaxing prayer. I've even taught my children to pray it when they have trouble falling asleep, so soothing is the intercession of our Blessed Mother. And have you ever heard the old assurance that your guardian angel will finish your rosary for you if you fall asleep? Cling to it in the sleep-deprived seasons of your life.
- "But I'm the mom of a newborn. I don't always *get* a shower." It's OK. Pray the rosary on the days you do get one. Or pray while you care for your baby.

- "But I can't pray in the car. It's too distracting." The car works for some people, but if it doesn't for you, find something else.

- "But I can't listen to Catholic radio or watch Catholic TV. We don't have them around here." Visit a Catholic bookstore and buy a CD of the rosary.

- "But I don't have a Catholic bookstore." Try the Internet. You can order anything online. Or download the rosary. There are lots of Web sites that offer it free. Do a search for "free audio download rosary."

- "But I don't have Internet access." Go to a library. Do a search online, and you'll find loads of Catholic booksellers that offer rosary books, CDs and even DVDs. Request catalogs, and get on some mailing lists. Soon your objection will be, "But I can't order any more of these great rosary resources. I've already spent too much."

I offer these final "get tough" retorts because I know all the "But I can't…" objections intimately. I've used a number of them myself.

I remember arguing with my spiritual director Father Joe that there was no reason for me to keep praying the rosary at my holy hour when all I seemed capable of was closing my eyes and snoring. I was the mother of a three-year-old who still hadn't slept through the night, and I was homeschooling my older daughters and trying to keep up with a number of other activities.

I'll never forget what my wise director said to me that day. I'm paraphrasing, but his message was, "So, you're sleepy. But you've been doing the work *he* gave you to do, and it's exhausting. So give him *that*. Give him your exhaustion if that's all that you have left. And if you fall asleep in church while you're trying to pray, it's OK. He'll know why."

Father Joe reminded me that in embracing my vocation, I was embracing another form of prayer—an active and exhausting form. But in persevering and continuing to give God everything (even my imperfect holy hour and rosary), I was offering him all I was capable of, even when that meant collapsing in his presence.

ONE STEP AT A TIME

Once we get past all the objections, we're ready to act. Here are a few final suggestions that can help you incorporate the rosary into your life one small step at a time.

A DECADE HERE AND THERE

If you still have trouble finding a fifteen-minute block for an entire rosary, try praying one decade at a time. Don't forget: It all counts. Prayer is prayer. Try a decade when you get up, one in the shower, another at lunch, one after dinner and one before you go to bed. Do that, and you've prayed a whole rosary.

PRAYER CHAINS

If your parish has a rosary prayer chain, sign yourself up. The way these usually work is that each person on the chain is assigned a mystery. When you're called on to pray for a specific intention, you pray one decade each day for a week or two, while others on the chain pray their decades, thus offering entire rosaries for the person who requested prayer. It's an easy way to start praying the rosary, and it keeps you accountable.

ON THE WAY TO MASS

What better way to assume a prayerful attitude for Mass than to pray the rosary beforehand? Pray a decade (or more, depending on the length of your drive) with your family on the way to church. If you've never done a family rosary, this is an easy way to start.

We began this with our daughters a few years ago, and now they hold us to that Sunday morning decade. If my husband and I are bickering over whether or not we closed the garage door, we're redirected by a loud but angelic chorus from the backseat, "Hey! We have to do our decade!"

PRAY WITH FRIENDS AND FAMILIES

Invite a few friends or entire families over to pray with you. Consider turning the gathering into a social time too. Some families have "Pizza and the Rosary" once a week. A friend in New York who is part of such a group observes, "This is absolutely, positively not a meditative rosary. There are children ranging in ages from 18 months (my twins) to college age. Our devotions could be considered more athletic than contemplative."[1]

Remember, it all counts. Even the athletic versions.

Other ideas for a friend-and-family rosary are gathering after Mass for prayer and potluck, hosting or helping with a moms' group that opens or closes meetings with a decade (or a full set of mysteries) or beginning your Bible study or other prayer group with the rosary.

MAKE AND PRAY

Another friend, a Nebraska mother of two, got her kids involved in the making of rosaries. Her family then donated the rosaries to missions or left them in the back of the church for people to pick up.

There are a number of books and Web sites that offer rosary-making instructions, from the easiest of knot-tying to more intricate methods involving techniques used in jewelry making. A search for "make a rosary" will yield a number of choices. Praying for a specific person on a homemade rosary and then giving that rosary as a gift can add special meaning.

I remember being particularly moved when a friend gave my husband a homemade rosary upon his reception into the Church. She told us she'd been praying for him for months with that very rosary.

VARY YOUR MEDITATIONS

My rosary-making friend also talks about a variation on her meditations. She likes to visualize the person for whom she's praying in the arms of Jesus or Mary. By focusing on specific intentions for conversion or healing, her meditations take on a new dimension and have a powerful intercessory component.

A Benedictine sister told me that when she has trouble sleeping, she will sometimes substitute a simple expression, such as "My Jesus, mercy," for a decade. Sister Marita is sure that Jesus doesn't mind getting such makeshift "roses."

AUDIO AND VISUAL AIDS

Some people are highly visual. Pictures of the mysteries can help them stay focused and on track with their prayer. There's a rich variety of rosary aids available, from books with simple drawings to those featuring reproductions of great art. Browse a bookstore or the Internet, and you're sure to find something that will help you meditate.

One of my favorite rosary books offers a different page and picture for every Hail Mary of the rosary, but I sometimes remain on the same page and meditate on one painting that speaks to me. Remember, this is *your* rosary. It's perfectly acceptable to do what you need to do to make it meaningful for you.

Books that list the Scripture citations for each mystery can be extremely helpful. (These are sometimes referred to as "scriptural rosaries," but that's a bit of a misnomer, since every rosary by its nature is a scriptural rosary.) Some people need to read only a single Scripture verse to ignite a string of meditations, while others prefer resources that offer more commentary. Eloquent reflection on Scripture is the perfect springboard for many and can lead to beautiful mental imagery.

When my husband (like me, a convert to the Catholic faith) first began praying the rosary, I gave him two of my favorite rosary recordings, assuming he'd love them as much as I do. They each offer a number of embellishments, such as musical interludes and short commentary. Though he was grateful for the encouragement and appreciated the sincerity of my efforts, he has found that what he likes best in an audio aid is a simple, straightforward recitation. Neither of us is wrong, of course. We simply have different tastes.

Whatever your style or preference, it's certain that there's a resource out there that can help you.

A Word About Praying With Children

Remember my friend's "athletic rosary"? Every parent has felt that way. Let's face it, praying with young children can feel like a wrestling match. It may even feel pointless.

Tom and I have found that training our children in prayer is an ongoing process. The good news is that children *do* learn. Praying with toddlers *will* bear fruit. We've had the privilege of watching our family prayer times advance from noisy affairs, during which we've said things like "Don't wrap that rosary around your toes" and "Stop hitting her," to more inspiring affairs during which we hear things like "Mommy, let's do the crowning of Mary!"

Push on through the storms of frustration, and one day the clouds will part, and you'll catch a glimpse of the radiant rainbow that is your child's developing prayer life.

chapter ten

TAKE HEART

A FINAL WORD ON PERSEVERANCE

[W]hen alone (I am ashamed to admit it) the recitation of the
rosary is more difficult for me than the wearing of an instrument
of penance.... I force myself in vain to meditate on the mysteries
of the rosary; I don't succeed in fixing my mind on them.

—SAINT THÉRÈSE OF LISIEUX[1]

Prayer is not about success and failure, but it does demand our
will. Prayer is a battle, and it's up to us to fight. Sometimes merely
showing up is half the battle.

Showing up is easy when everything is going well. When our
schedules allow it, when spiritual consolations are rolling in, when
sleep is consistent and our health is good, when work is effortless
and none of our kids are at a difficult stage, then it's a breeze to
keep our end of the bargain. It's the trying times, the crises big
and small, that test our commitment.

Continuing to show up for prayer when it's dry or inconven-
ient, when all we can manage is two Hail Marys before we fall
asleep, when we're out of work or in financial trouble, when we
are doubting, sick, sad or lonely, when we've lost someone we
love—those are the trials that test our mettle. When we keep

praying through the misery, giving God all that we're capable of, no matter how inadequate that seems, he will reward us. He will accept our meager offering and transform it into something exquisite.

It may be that we'll feel just enough peace to sleep (or that a child finally does), we're given a moment of comfort and courage after the death of a loved one, or we suddenly, firmly know we have the strength to be open to life and accept the baby who is on the way. Whatever message he sends, we can be sure that it is a part of that continual conversation that is known as prayer. The conversation can only continue when we're talking too.

A WEIGHTY ISSUE

I'd be remiss if I didn't say more about distractions in prayer. We are fallen creatures, and one of the traps we fall into is distraction from the things of God. When the distractions come, as they always will, how should we handle them?

First of all, take heart and thank God for distractions. Yes, thank him! Our distractions will show us "what we are attached to" (*CCC*, 2729), and that is a good rather than a discouraging thing. As the *Catechism* says, "this humble awareness before the Lord should awaken our preferential love for him and lead us resolutely to offer him our heart to be purified. Therein lies the battle, the choice of which master to serve" (*CCC*, 2729).

A distraction helps us see more clearly where our hearts lie. And once we see that, we can do battle, breaking down false attachments and turning our hearts back to God.

But breaking down attachments is easier said than done. We may resolve, "I won't let work distract me today," but how do we implement that resolution?

There's no painless shortcut. It's simply something we must *do*. Again and again and again.

It's a lot like losing weight. We want a magical answer, the perfect diet, the right pill. But the reality is that we have to eat less and exercise more, as annoying as that reality is. With prayer we must mentally wander less and pray more. That might sound as irritating as the weight-loss advice, but it's true. The moment we realize that our minds are beginning to wander, we have to drag them back, reject the distracting thoughts and redirect our minds to prayer. When the next distraction pops up, we do it again. Wander less. Pray more.

A friend of mine says that she gets so distracted when she tries to pray the rosary and is so crippled by her level of attention deficit that she simply cannot get through an entire rosary. She wonders if there is any hope for "someone like her."

Admittedly, some people do get more distracted in prayer (and in life) than others. A genuine problem with attention span makes meditation difficult and challenging. For some it's a cross they will carry all their lives. But in general I think we all face similar struggles in the battle for prayer. We assume everyone else is doing swimmingly, that we're the only ones who can't pay attention. But if prayer were easy, there'd be no need to call it a battle. The distractible few would be an exception, when in reality distraction is the rule. So take heart—you're not alone.

Saint Thérèse of Lisieux, a doctor of the Church, understood distraction. In particular she knew how it felt to wrestle with the rosary. Fortunately she was a realist: She knew that she was a fallen human being. She came to accept her limitations and didn't abandon prayer.

Thérèse learned that sometimes "just showing up" was all she could offer:

> For a long time I was desolate about this lack of devotion
> which astonished me, for *I love the* Blessed Virgin so much
> that it should be easy for me to recite in her honor prayers
> which are so pleasing to her. Now I am less desolate; I think
> that the Queen of heaven, since she is *my MOTHER,* must
> see my good will and she is satisfied with it.[2]

I believe Saint Thérèse was right: The Blessed Mother was pleased
with her imperfect efforts. Jesus knows our weaknesses too. He
knows when we're doing our best, even if our best appears to be
failure. If half the battle for prayer is "just showing up," then
Thérèse fought valiantly. We can do the same.

Sometimes the result is nothing more than a resigned feeling
of duty, but occasionally the reward will be sublime beyond
imagining. And we can't make room for the sublime if we don't
show up.

REAL PRAYER

If we dwell on our distractions, we might be tempted toward a
whole new batch of "But I can'ts." We might think, "But I can't
call this *prayer*; I'm not paying attention." Reject that temptation,
and know that there are different levels and depths of prayer, just
as there are different levels in other kinds of communication.

Consider the wide variety of conversations you have every
day with someone you love. Let's use a spouse as an example. In
the morning there may be a quick, utilitarian talk about plans.
During the day you might check in with each other briefly. Over
dinner you catch up a bit. Perhaps once a week, on "date night,"
you get out of the house, away from distractions, and *really* talk.
You reconnect at a deeper level, and you're reminded of just how
much you love this person.

Though the levels of communication differ, the quick morning talk is no less "real" than is the lingering, intimate exchange. Your interactions vary in quality, but all are important, and all are real, legitimate components of the relationship that is marriage.

The same is true in our relationship with God. Unless we are cloistered religious (priests, monks or nuns who belong to orders whose charism is contemplative prayer), we cannot sit in contemplation all day. That doesn't mean we can't "pray always," but we must pray in a different manner, in a way that is compatible with an active life in the world. God understands that sometimes the conversation will be quick and utilitarian, while at other times it will be that lingering, intimate exchange.

We are and always will be distracted in prayer: It's part of the human predicament. Distraction in prayer is a microcosm of distraction in life. The world is full of activities, people, ideas and things that threaten to pull us away from God. Earthly concerns, from the vital and necessary to the mundane and meaningless, consume our thoughts, drawing us away from the spiritual life or tempting us to sin. The same is true in prayer: Distractions pull us from God. All we can do is persevere, repeatedly redirecting our hearts and minds back to where they belong: with God.

Our Blessed Mother is praying for us to have that perseverance, and our loving Father knows how hard we're trying. Like the father who watches his son ride a bike for the first time, God knows why we weave and wobble, and he watches the shaky results of our perseverance with abundant joy for our trying.

So take heart. He's waiting for us at the end of the street.

"Rejoice always, pray constantly, give thanks in all circumstances, for this is the will of God in Christ Jesus for you" (1 Thessalonians 5:16–18).

CONCLUSION

Initially I said that I hoped to make a convincing case for the rosary, clear up a few misunderstandings and offer some practical tips for praying it. I hope, by God's grace, that I've been able to do that. But most of all I hope that what's reached out to you from these pages is the steadfast teaching of the Catholic Church, the trusted guidance of the popes, who are our spiritual fathers, the edifying wisdom of the saints, the prayers and the care of our Blessed Mother, the Word of God in Scripture and the love of Jesus Christ.

Compelling arguments and practical tips can take us only so far. In the end everything about which the Catholic Church teaches us, and that includes the rosary, comes down to this: Who do we say that he is (see Mark 8:29)?

May your prayers, and especially the rosary, lead you to Jesus.

> For this reason I bow my knees before the Father, from whom every family in heaven and on earth is named, that according to the riches of his glory he may grant you to be strengthened with might through his Spirit in the inner man, and that Christ may dwell in your hearts through faith; that you, being rooted and grounded in love, may have power to comprehend with all the saints what is the breadth and length and height and depth, and to know the love of Christ which surpasses knowledge, that you may be filled with all the fulness of God. (Ephesians 3:14–19)

Notes

CHAPTER ONE: A SAFE PORT

1. Quoted in Pope John Paul II, *Rosarium Virginis Mariae*, Apostolic Letter on the Most Holy Rosary, October 16, 2002, no. 43, available at: www.vatican.va.
2. Ann M. Brown, *Apostle of the Rosary: Blessed Bartolo Longo* (New Hope, Ky.: New Hope, 2004), p. 53.
3. John Paul II, Angelus message, October 29, 1978, available at: www.vatican.va.

CHAPTER TWO: THE ROSARY: ITS ORIGINS AND ITS MIRACLES

1. See Guy Bedouelle, *Saint Dominic: The Grace of the Word*, Mary Thomas Noble, O.P., trans. (San Francisco: Ignatius, 1987), p. 253.
2. Bedouelle, p. 255.
3. See Bedouelle, p. 253.
4. See Bedouelle, p. 255.
5. See Bedouelle, pp. 256–257.
6. Bedouelle, p. 257.
7. Pope Benedict XVI, Angelus message of Sunday, October 2, 2007, available at: www.vatican.va.
8. Michael Walsh, ed., *Butler's Lives of the Saints*, concise ed. (San Francisco: Harper & Row, 1985), p. 129.
9. Pope Pius IX, quoted at http://rosary.prayer.googlepages.com.

CHAPTER THREE: BEYOND WORDS

1. C.S. Lewis, *Letters to Malcolm, Chiefly on Prayer* (Orlando, Fla.: Harcourt, 1992), p. 5.
2. *Rosarium Virginis Mariae*, 36.

3. *Rosarium Virginis Mariae*, 2. The pope was quoting his own Angelus message of October 29, 1978.

CHAPTER FOUR: HAIL MARY

1. *Rosarium Virginis Mariae*, 36.
2. *Cathechism of the Catholic Church*, (Washington, D.C.: USCCB, 1997), p. 904.

CHAPTER FIVE: THE MOTHER'S PLACE

1. See "Pray Rosary for Peace, Benedict XVI Urges," October 7, 2007, available at: http://www.zenit.org.
2. *Rosarium Virginis Mariae*, 40.
3. *Rosarium Virginis Mariae*, 11.

CHAPTER SIX: DON'T WORRY: THE MECHANICS OF THE ROSARY

1. See www.ewtn.com for the Litany of Loreto.

CHAPTER SEVEN: "LEARNING HIM": THE MYSTERIES OF THE ROSARY

1. *Rosarium Virginis Mariae*, 38.
2. *Rosarium Virginis Mariae*, 20.
3. *Rosarium Virginis Mariae*, 21.

CHAPTER NINE: MAKING IT WORK

1. Mary Ellen Barrett, "Families That Pray Together," *Long Island Catholic*, March 5, 2008.

CHAPTER TEN: TAKE HEART: A FINAL WORD ON PERSEVERANCE

1. John Clarke, O.C.D., trans., *Story of a Soul: The Autobiography of St. Thérèse of Lisieux* (Washington, D.C.: ICS, 1976), p. 242.
2. *Story of a Soul,* pp. 242–243.